Cloudhand

CLENCHED FIST

Cloudhand

CLENCHED FIST

CHAOS,
CRISIS,
AND THE
EMERGENCE
OF
COMMUNITY

RHEA Y. MILLER

LuraMedia, Inc.
7060 Miramar Rd., Suite 104
San Diego, CA 92121

Cover design by Dan Tollas, Philadelphia, PA
Cover calligraphy by Sara Steele, Philadelphia, PA
Printed on Recycled Paper

Library of Congress Cataloging-in-Publication Data
Miller, Rhea Y., date.
    Cloudhand, clenched fist : chaos, crisis, and the emergence of community /
Rhea Y. Miller.
        p.   cm.
    Includes bibliographical references and index.
    ISBN 1-880913-19-4 (pbk.)
    1. Paradigm (Theory of knowledge)   2. Paradigms (Social sciences)
3. Paradox.   4. Chaos (Christian theology)   I. Title.
BD225.M55   1996   96-16368
191—dc20   CIP

A word about the front cover:
    The Chinese character Chun, according to the *I Ching*, means "difficulty at the
beginning. This hexagram is composed of K'an (rain) and Chen (thunder) . . . their
interaction describes the 'teaming chaotic profusion' which creates multiple
possibilities. . . . We are at the dynamic moment in which an inner-world change
is beginning to precipitate into an outer-world change."
—*A Guide to the I Ching, Third Edition Revised and Expanded*
    by Carol K. Anthony, Anthony Publishing Company, 1988. (Reprinted by permission)

Grateful acknowledgment is made for permission to reprint copyrighted material:

Quotation from *Jamestown Commitment* by Owanah Anderson. Reprinted by
    permission of Forward Movement Publications.
Quotations from *A Timeless Way of Building* by Christopher Alexander. Copyright ©
    1979 by Christopher Alexander. Reprinted by permission of Oxford University
    Press.
Quotation from *Angels Fear: Towards an Epistemology of the Sacred* by Gregory
    Bateson and Mary Catherine Bateson. Copyright ©1987 by the Estate of Gregory
    Bateson and Mary Catherine Bateson. Reprinted with the permission of Simon &
    Schuster.
Quotation from *Wishful Thinking: A Seeker's ABC* by Frederick Buechner. Copyright
    ©1973 by Frederick Buechner. Reprinted by permission of HarperCollins
    Publishers, Inc.
Quotation from *Belonging to the Universe* by Fritjof Capra and David Steindl-Rast.
    Copyright ©1991 by Fritjof Capra and David Steindl-Rast. Reprinted by
    permission of HarperCollins Publishers, Inc.

'Tis the gift to be simple,
'Tis the gift to be free,
'Tis the gift to come down where we ought to be.
And when we find ourselves in the place just right,
'Twill be in the valley of love and delight.
When true simplicity is gained,
To bow and to bend we shan't be ashamed,
To turn, turn will be our delight
'Till by turning, turning we come round right.

— Traditional Shaker Song

CONTENTS

ILLUSTRATIONS

ACKNOWLEDGMENTS

First and foremost, I offer great gratitude to my partner, Sandy Bishop, who sustained me body and soul in every aspect of daily living while I struggled to get this book out.

I also give heartfelt thanks to:

Charley Musselman, for helping me enter the computer world and offering sound advice as a physicist and friend;

Anne Rousseau, who rescued my computer disk of the first draft of the manuscript from fire and flood;

John Butler, who continued to believe in me and who, as a true friend does, sang my song back to me at those times when I had forgotten it;

The Episcopal Divinity School, which gave me the first opportunity to put a draft manuscript together;

Both the publisher and editor of LuraMedia for making this work reader-friendly and challenging me to be even clearer in my communication;

Neil Hanson for the illustration "Two Profiles";

Charles Black for his technical assistance with the Mandelbrot Set illustrations;

The readers of my manuscript drafts, each of whose insights I took very seriously (even those whose challenges were a bit painful);

All my friends who supported me along the way and dealt with my preoccupation;

All the writers upon whom I have drawn support;

And finally, to all the people with vision who dare to act on it.

I could weave you a tapestry of myriad colors to show you the intricacy of the universe, but the worldview of the new sciences is so extraordinary that such a tapestry would not be enough. Though some tapestries invite you to touch, and others allow you to look deep within, they are still basically two-dimensional. It is all too easy to remain unaffected by the tapestry, to stay "in control," to concentrate on the simplicity of the warp and the woof, a set of coordinates for the ordered mind. In short, it would be too easy to maintain your present worldview.

AN

INVITATION

TO

HEART

AND

MIND

Rather than write this book as if I were weaving you a tapestry, I have written as if I were building you a house. I did this once in the woods of a northern sea island. The advantage of a house over a tapestry is that you can walk into it, experience the furnishings, sit awhile if you like, touch, smell, have your mood changed—and perhaps have your worldview challenged. And though I have built a house, and know that certain steps come first, I have also learned that the secret of carpentry is not doing everything right, precise, and correct the first time, though God knows we try; rather, we must learn how to creatively correct or compensate for each and every unexpected mistake.

I admit that I take artistic license in my attempt to build this house for you. I do not know the exact order of the construction of this particular house, nor the exact dimensions. Though the house is three-dimensional, I use it to point to a reality that may be four, five, or more dimensions. The amazing cosmologist Stephen Hawking goes so far as to assert that there may be no beginning and no end, no boundary to the universe at all.[1] The task of describing what is so truly awesome is difficult indeed.

A philosopher has differentiated two ways of knowing: ". . . theoretic, which is scientifically verifiable, and aesthetic, which is immediately apprehensible. Complete knowledge requires a synthesis of the two."[2] This is my bias in *Cloudhand, Clenched Fist*. I bring all of my rational ability to this work. However, I also bring my art, with the awareness that my art may indeed inform better than my rational presentation.

For instance, when reading several of the new cosmology theories, I kept getting an image of something concave against something convex. I saw an image of a balloon or bubble, with one universe being what was enveloped inside of that bubble, and the other defined by the outside of that envelope, which itself was another envelope. I could make no rational sense out of this image, but I did get a "sense" of something. Later, a friend brought me an article from *Science* by David Freedman about the most recent correction to the inflation theory of the cosmos

> . . . in which the newborn universe goes through an episode . . . analogous to the boiling of a liquid. As steam appears as bubbles in water, a new phase of the universe emerged as expanding bubbles. Outside the bubbles was a hot soup of massless particles in which the direction of time was ill-defined, while inside the bubbles were matter and time much as we know them. . . .

> Eureka, went the thinking: All the matter in our universe is simply a relic of processes in those short-lived bubble walls.[3]

Do not panic. I do not fully comprehend this quote nor the cosmological theory behind it either, but I am aware that my intuition is a valuable source of insight and a source of my art. Intuition offers a door of access to understanding that is distinct from strictly scientific or mathematical discourse. So, I ask you to trust your own intuition as you read.

This book is not for the faint of heart. It challenges many of today's assumptions, some considered sacred. Experience shows us, however, that we do not risk entering a new worldview without first possessing some form of faith and hope. As an old mentor of mine, a French worker priest named Alain Richard, once said to me, "You must look for the signs of hope. And if you look, I guarantee you will find them."

Finally, this is a book written for the heart. I have not neglected the mind, but I am aware that the mind is so powerful and can be so tyrannical that, unless I address the heart, the mind may keep the heart hidden away. The mind without the heart is free to engage in fanciful and cruel deeds. In order to address the heart, this book will involve you in ways that are more demanding than other, more familiar theoretical reading. I ask you to participate with me in walking through this house. I do not offer you a grid to show you where you should place your foot each and every step through this house. Instead, I encourage and invite you to seek your own tour.

I must caution you to remember that I point to what is just now breaking through into my own consciousness, and into that of others, many much more scientific than I. I see this awesome house only in glimpses, through signs and dreams. It is more than a house, really—a temple, or perhaps the Temple, which originally, in certain faiths, was nothing more than a tent in the desert . . .

*W*hen growing up, my mother would walk into a room and say, "This place looks like chaos!" I wasn't sure what it meant then, but I thought chaos had to do with messiness, since house-cleaning was the inevitable result of such a statement. I also thought chaos must mean something bad because the next statement was always, "What if the bishop would drop by?" Since my father was a minister, the potential arrival of the hierarch was the ever-present threat dictating the need for tidiness, cleanliness, and orderliness.

In cultures such as mine, particularly those of Jewish/Christian heritage, "chaos" is a dreaded word. The Hebraic traditional image of chaos is that of a huge sea monster, the leviathan or whale that must be confined to the deep recesses of the sea. God's role, according to Hebrew scholar Jon Levenson, is to engage constantly on our behalf in the battle of order over chaos, or evil. Levenson conceives of God not so much as attempting to eliminate evil as to confine it. In this tradition, we must implore God to continue this battle on our behalf or we will perish; if

CLOUDHAND,
CLENCHED
FISTS,
COMMUNITY,
AND
CRISIS

God abandons the world, chaos will reign.[1] From this perspective, chaos is a frightening prospect.

From the more neutral mathematical perspective, chaos is simply the result of certain nonlinear equations, equations that cannot be divided evenly. There is always a remainder that is ever changing. There is no tidy end to nonlinear equations. I remember as a student being irritated by those division problems that failed to resolve beyond the decimal point.

For instance, take a chaotic nonlinear equation such as $x = c - x^2$, where $c = .4$ to 2. Do not let the mathematical complexity of this equation alarm you. Simply note that this equation is self-referential, and "x" must be replaced by the answer each time. In other words, a chaotic nonlinear equation constantly circles back on itself.

To get a feel for the difference between a chaotic nonlinear equation and a linear equation, imagine taking a trip. If you set your destination, get an AAA guidebook, and follow the guidelines to reach your destination, this would be something like working with a linear equation. However, if you travel without a set destination and use an AAA guidebook only to inform you about where you find yourself at any given moment, not to take you to a particular point, this would be more like working with a chaotic nonlinear equation. Such a nonlinear trip would involve travel for the sake of travel, with endless new vistas and new experiences, yet never arriving at an end point.

Edward Lorenz, a research meteorologist (i.e., weatherman), discovered a unique phenomenon when studying certain nonlinear equations, or chaos. Imagine a butterfly's wings—a favorite, perhaps the monarch or the common blue—and simplify the shape in your mind. This is a portrayal of what is called the "Lorenz attractor" (see Figure 1). It is a computer-generated image of a chaotic system that

> ... never exactly repeats itself, [and] the trajectory never intersects itself. Instead it loops around and around forever. ... it traces a strange, distinctive shape, a kind of double spiral in three dimensions, like a butterfly with its two wings.[2]

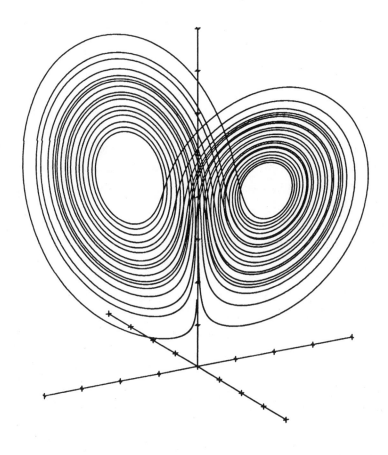

Figure 1. Lorenz Attractor.

James P. Crutchfield/Adolph E. Brotman. From *Chaos* by James Gleick. Reprinted by permission.

This image of chaos as a butterfly has a vastly different feel to it than the traditional Hebraic image of chaos as a sea monster. Because the Greek word for "butterfly" carries the same root meaning as the word "soul," there would have been an enormous difference in connotation for the concept of chaos among the Greeks if they had visualized chaos as a butterfly rather than a sea monster. Our images of words tell us much about their meaning for our culture.

Move to yet another image from a different culture. Imagine a *t'ai chi* master practicing at dawn by a stream in China. *T'ai chi chuan*, a discipline similar in form to dance, is a sacred ritual used to center the practitioner with the elemental forces at work in the universe. The movement is the basis of the contemporary martial arts and various forms of *t'ai chi*. *T'ai chi* uses complementary circles where energy ("*chi*") is understood never to be lost but to circle constantly back upon itself. The breathing of the earth is an example of this flow of energy: Plants breathe in carbon dioxide and out oxygen, humans breathe in the oxygen and out carbon dioxide, and the cycle continues as the plants breathe the CO_2 back in.

The *t'ai chi* master moves slowly, revolving and stretching in movements so fluid as to make one marvel that she is restricted to the same two arms, two legs, and spinal axis as we are. Imagine watching such a master and being filled, as is the master, with a profound peace, a profound sense of harmony. Imagine further being lost for some time in the beauty of the *t'ai chi* movement that has gone on morning after morning, age dawning upon age. For whatever reason—perhaps out of the Western tendency for analysis—you notice that the master's movements, though never following in exactly the same circles, form a pattern resembling the wings of a butterfly. The movement is known as the Cloudhand.[*] If the movements of the hands of the Cloudhand practitioner were to be traced on a piece of paper, an image would appear very similar to the Lorenz attractor!

As a child, an aspiring *t'ai chi* master (I'll call her Sadako) watched other masters—from a discreet distance, of course. She

---

[*]   "The Cloudhand is basically a movement that stirs up your tant'ien [core—envisioned in the abdominal area] energy upward and outward and then circles back. If we cut an apple in half, we see two smaller circles overlapping in the center. Your spine is like the core and your arm motion is like the two overlapping circles. Each hand, in turn, scoops up energy from the tant'ien and rises up the center line of your chest before turning outward, revolving, sinking downward, and curving back to the tant'ien. Then the other hand picks up the motion of the first and goes through the same cycle. Your torso pivots to follow the hand as it turns and revolves outward and downward." (Huang, Chungliang Al. *Embrace Tiger, Return to Mountain: The Essence of Tai Ji*. Berkeley, CA: Celestial Arts, 1987, 41-42.)

had practiced in private, clumsily and yet so faithfully. At some point Sadako must have noticed she had all the movements memorized. Her technique was flawless. But something was missing. For weeks?/months?/years? she struggled, and yet her flawless technique conveyed only precision, accuracy, and discipline, while a master radiated a fluidity, harmony, and beauty that transformed the very being of even those who watched.

Sadako did not know when it happened, whether it was the morning she grieved the loss of her little brother, or the day she heard the stream talk for the first time, or the day she forgot to notice her own self. What she did remember was the day she noticed other children watching her with those same awe-struck eyes with which she had watched her master. Furthermore, she realized these children were not simply seeing her but were glimpsing something much greater than she, something of the soul of the universe.

There are dance schools in the United States that put footprints on the floor for beginners to copy. There is an attention to detail, the positioning of particular steps. As long as the dancer is confined to this understanding, there may be a technical mastery, but the onlooker still perceives a sense of stiffness. There is more of an awareness of the individual steps than the whole of the dance. However, when the dancer begins to relate to the movement as a pattern, and to resonate in relationship with the pattern rather than the details, then a fluidity and aliveness in the dance occurs. The audience perceives a sense of soulfulness in the dancer.

In the "step-by-step" mindset, the goal is a specific set of movements to be conquered and completed. In the "pattern" mindset, the point is the continuous journey of dance that resonates with an awareness of being part of something greater, of being in relationship. The ability to replicate the exact components of dance, or of *t'ai chi*, does not constitute mastery. The masters are able to do something far more. They develop an ability to enter into a relationship of endless possibility within some sort of spiritual awareness that engages the very nature of the universe.[3]

Like a dance pattern or Cloudhand movement, the chaos of the world can be seen as a pattern of endless possibilities in harmony somehow with the soul of the universe, rather than as a threatening or frightening endless nightmare of a sea monster that we must fight against. This constitutes a very different mindset from what most of us experience today. Currently, the predominant way of looking at the world is known either as the "Newtonian worldview," named after Isaac Newton, or the "Cartesian worldview," named after René Descartes. Proponents of this worldview believe the world is divisible into discernible individual building blocks, set in motion at some point of creation, whose sum constitutes the whole of our present world.

The Newtonian worldview values hierarchy, categorization, orderliness, and "either/or" propositions. Everything has a name and a place. Something is either right or wrong, up or down, in or out. The "win/lose" dichotomy is part of this mindset. This worldview sees the universe as a giant clock composed of intricately connected individual parts. This clock is widely believed to be the result of chance, of endless trial and error. In short, there is no necessity for a spiritual awareness in the Newtonian perspective.

Prior to the Newtonian worldview, however, there was no distinction between science and religion, the former being only one aspect of the latter. Science was a vehicle for expressing religious truth about the universe as much as religion was a vehicle for science. For instance, in the Jewish/Christian culture, healing used to be a matter for priests, since illness was believed to be the result of sin, not disease. Over time, this approach resulted in some very troubling dilemmas.

When science postulated that the earth was not the center of the universe, the dominant religion in the Western world took this as a personal affront to its sovereignty and denounced science. Scientists, or healers who defied the Church, were branded as heretics or witches and were excommunicated, even executed. For a while, Christianity controlled the direction of science and obstructed any scientific progress that might lead to conclusions different from what the Christian Church wanted the public to believe. For this reason, science found it necessary to divorce itself from religion. Out of this separation, the Newtonian worldview emerged. The Newtonian worldview was a blessing for its time: It brought us modern transportation, telecommunications, and all the contemporary amenities of daily living. But the disastrous, unforeseen result of the split between science and religion was that science went on to posit that knowledge existed separate of any moral or ethical realm, that the ethical consequences of scientific endeavors were not an issue for science.

In 1981, during the forty days of the Christian season of Lent, I meditated at Camp Desert Rock in the Nevada Test Site. Across the ridge, twenty-five to thirty years before, soldiers chosen for their proven ability in combat had been put in trenches and told to cover their eyes while a nuclear blast had been detonated. The soldiers had then been marched under the nuclear mushroom clouds to see what psychological and physical effects resulted. They returned to Camp Desert Rock and, among other symptoms, began to vomit from radiation sickness and endure bouts of diarrhea. The scientists conducting the experiments had kept themselves at safe distance from the nuclear blasts under shielded conditions. But the soldiers had not been aware of the radiation danger. Careful and detailed records were kept of their condition but later were reported destroyed.

At the time I was meditating in their former encampment, nuclear testing continued, but underground. Certain survivors of the above-ground testing were just beginning to protest their treatment as human guinea pigs and were seeking compensation for their resulting illnesses. Today, newspapers are finally starting to question the responsibility and role of scientists regarding such human damage. The scientists at the test site, claiming they were just doing their individual jobs, as required of them, exhibited the classic Newtonian view that scientific knowledge is a separate, individual construct unrelated to moral and ethical considerations, much less spiritual considerations. Science, in that system, has no accountability to society.

Science was, and is, so preoccupied with specificity, with details, that it has almost become impossible to see the forest for the trees. As a result, much of the traditional scientific community, along with their devotees, remains immobilized, wrapped in the false security of their separate, individual, and isolated "techno-cocoons," unable to contribute substantially to solving the crises of our day.

Crisis often precipitates change, and change is the name of

the game in our lifetime. Scientist and novelist C. P. Snow calls attention to the fact that years ago time passed so slowly that an entire lifetime would not produce any noticeable change. Today, however, change is happening so rapidly that even our imagination cannot keep pace with it.[4] Yet, for many people and institutions, change is synonymous with insecurity. Fear surrounds change. Understandably, the more changes we experience, the more we may resist change.

As one of my history teachers once stated, the more unstable a culture or institution, the more conservative it becomes. In an age where people are holding on for dear life, where people are filled with the fear of impending destruction of all that is familiar and dear to them, whether from war, poverty, or environmental disaster, it is no surprise to find so much resistance, so many clenched fists. People clench ever more tightly to old familiar ways and fight what they do not understand. This is demonstrated vividly in the current revival of worldwide militant religious fundamentalism, whether Buddhist, Jewish, Christian, or Muslim. Fascism is also once again on the rise, either as "ethnic-cleansing," "neo-nazism," or peasant genocide. As people struggle fiercely with feelings of powerlessness against change and search valiantly for solid ground, violence becomes exponential. Unfortunately, too many people operate under the cultural myth that survival depends upon supreme weaponry and the ability to dominate over any enemies[5]—even the "enemy" of change.

In recent years there has been a burgeoning change in the field of the "new sciences"—such as the new physics, new cosmology, new biology—that has ramifications for all of us. Amazing discoveries, especially in the field of physics, have brought into question the Newtonian mechanistic worldview and suggest a radically different possibility. The new sciences posit that, rather than a universe made of individual building blocks, our universe is built primarily of space, waves of energy, and electrical charge. These scientists are seeing the universe as composed of probable patterns of relationships that may emerge into more complex patterns, with the whole being greater than the sum of its parts. This new-science worldview is as different from the Newtonian worldview as performing the Cloudhand motion is from following footprints on a dance studio floor.

The new sciences say that society has been living under several false premises, one of which has been used to justify violence. "Might makes right" has been a slogan buttressed by the evolutionary premise of the survival of the fittest. The new biology contends that evolution was never a matter of the survival of the fittest. In fact, biologists Lynn Margulis and Dorion Sagan have discovered that the earth's ability to evolve came about via constant mutual cooperation and networking, not by warfare.[6] This suggests, then, that *survival came within the context of, and is dependent upon, community.* Clenched fists, a sign of "might," are a notion of the past, a concept of rigidity—itself a sign of impending extinction.

This cooperative rather than competitive new worldview also suggests that science does not stand alone—isolated, unencumbered by moral or ethical or even spiritual considerations. Even more radically, it suggests that *each of us does not stand alone.* Surviving the crises of our everyday lives, caused by the relentless pace of change in our world, demands this kind of radical transformation in our worldview. This is not to suggest that we destroy what we know. But rather, we put our old "science" into new perspective. We can enter a new dimension of understanding that goes beyond our current comprehension.

This is small comfort for people with power in the prevailing worldview. The fear of traditional scientists, for example, when confronted with the new sciences, is that history will repeat itself and religious institutions will again attain inordinate control over the rest of society and prevent the pursuit of true scientific endeavor.[7] For these scientists, the new sciences represent a return to magical and superstitious understanding, which have nothing to do with real science, or "hard science."[8] They point with disgust at New Age adherents, considering them irresponsible, unable to face squarely the dilemmas of the current world without resorting to spirituality as a crutch. The perceived threat of the new sciences is so great to some that, although the data from the new sciences has been available (some of it for more than seventy years), it is not yet taught to our children.

The words of the German scientist Max Planck offer a spine-tingling warning:

> . . . a new scientific truth does not triumph by con-
> vincing its opponents and making them see the
> light, but rather because its opponents eventually
> die, and a new generation grows up that is familiar
> with it.[9]

At the pace of the current crises, we may not live to see that generation in place.

Every human institution in existence today, whether politi-cal, social, scientific, or religious, perceives a change of under-standing as a threat. These institutions constitute staggering resistance to the very hope of our survival. Yet if we continue to resort to clenched fists as a means of coping with change, the challenge would be overwhelming.

As a social justice activist, I often encounter clenched fists. I have spent considerable time on the streets with the citizens of America, Japan, Israel, and Mexico, and I have encountered much fear and resistance to change. I have agonized with people bereft of the assistance of the scientific, religious, economic, and political institutions of their communities.

As a woman, I have experienced how difficult and complex is the web of social factors involved in a change of worldview along gender lines alone, much less a total worldview change.

As one who has been trained as a priest, I have seen the power of letting go of clenched fists and of opening the heart—not in the churches of the world but in the streets. I have seen firsthand how we in the Western world are experiencing nothing short of a crisis of belief.

It is ironic that, at the very time the institutions so resistant to change continue to isolate themselves, little pockets of people are sprouting up all over the world with energy to tackle the seemingly impossible. Unnoticed, unseen, at the margins, on the periphery of many cultures, people are building relationships with one another in ways that are so empowering as to defy explanation. People are moving to a new dimension of understanding that is chock full of creativity. There is a vitality and aliveness in the midst of the most dire circumstances. I firmly believe the new sciences model is an opening for us to this new understanding of empowered community, but it demands a level of commitment—dare I even say faith—quite foreign to us. Furthermore, even with the new understanding, like the child watching the master, there is no substitute for the practice of it. We can understand and think correctly all we want, but until we actually practice the dance or *t'ai chi* Cloudhand movement, over and over again, will it come alive for us.

I have done a bit of this dancing myself, though not alone. It is through my experience of dancing chaos with other committed men, women, and children that I have become convinced we are already well on the path to the emergence and empowerment of community on a level never seen before. It is not easy. It is not a foregone conclusion, but it is exciting, and it is awesome, and it is possible.

PARADOX

AND

PARADIGMS

I started out traditionally enough. My father was a circuit Methodist preacher in rural Iowa. I attended high school in a county seat town of 6500. I entered a small private college in Nebraska and worked my first full-time job in the downtown bank until classes started. By the time I was a sophomore, I had been elected student body president. That year I was invited to Washington, D.C., for the "President to Presidents" Conference. The President of the United States was to speak to the presidents of student bodies from all across the country.

We were all in for a surprise. This was 1970. President Nixon decided he could not speak with us after all. That left the vice-president, which would have suited me, but he declared we were all snobs, so we did not meet Spiro Agnew either. That left the cabinet. We met with Dean, Haldeman, Erlichman, etc. The only person I met who did not later end up in jail was Ruckelshouse. That was also the year Kent State happened. It was on my twentieth birthday. You could say the world was turning upside-down. You can count on the fact that I learned to question authority.

I knew things were out of kilter, but I did not have any sense of a different worldview. I was just shaken like everybody else. It was truly a time of classic clenched fists. Some people were violent in their response. Others were lost.

Upon graduation, I wandered from job to job, exploring the world through the eyes of "ordinary" people in ways I had not before allowed myself. I performed in a rock band, worked in K-Mart, and even did a stint as a dump truck driver. After three years, I returned to academia, this time to a liberal Christian seminary. During that first quarter back in school, some dear friends invited me to a lecture by a local feminist on feminist theory. I was not too keen on the idea of attending another lecture, especially one that would take up an evening—and by a feminist at that. I was among those who considered feminism a frivolous effort when compared to the weightier matters of the world, such as hunger, war, justice. I had a deep respect for these friends, however, and in deference to them, I attended the lecture.

The lecture was in a church building of some sort, an inexpensive site open to the public. As I sat there listening to this woman speak, I became aware of a subtle shift happening inside me. All of a sudden I had a sense that my world changed color. My whole world "turned" somehow. It was as if I had been looking at a picture and seeing an image defined by closed lines, when the real picture was to be found in the relationship of space around those closed lines. I had been seeing a chalice and had missed the image of two profiles facing each other (see Figure 2).

Until then, I had prioritized definition over description, individuals or events over relationships and community, "either/or" thinking over "both/and" awareness, truth-as-science over truth-as-story. The more I listened to this woman, the by now oft-quoted feminist and author Anne Wilson Schaef, the more the world made sense to me somehow. I experienced a resonance deep in my soul; I felt "at home" with what I was hearing. I knew I would never be the same again. It is the clearest example in my life of a worldview change, of a paradigm shift.

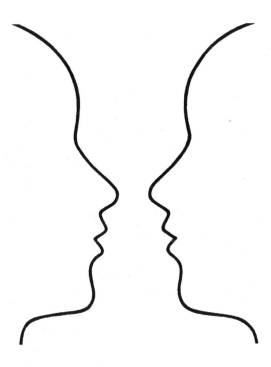

Figure 2. Two Profiles.

"Paradigm shift" is a word meant to convey the changing of the way we view the world: the turning or shifting of our perceptions, our overall concept of reality. It is not so much a matter of a change in the *content* of our world as it is a shift in our *understanding*. It is not so much a change of pitch on a musical scale, as a change in tone. It is not so much a change in shape, as a change in how the same shapes fit together. It is not the fact that the images in a picture change, but that the color of the entire picture changes. It is how the facts fall into a new place for us. A paradigm shift is the turning of the wheel in a kaleidoscope, where the same shapes produce an entirely new picture.

That night there were no new words in my vocabulary. I was not seeing anything that had not existed before. But for the first time, the way things fit together looked entirely different to me. It was as if my world had changed to living color.

It is important to understand that a paradigm shift is not a matter of seeing things more clearly. Rather, it is like perceiving the universe in a different color. It is not like using a microscope or better eye glasses or a cleaner window so we can perceive more detail. It is, instead, an entirely different way of seeing—or knowing. It is as if there is a series of rotating lights at the base of a Christmas tree that cast a sequence of different colors on the tree—first green, then red, then blue. Much is the same, yet everything is different.

A paradigm shift is a dimensional change. As human creatures, we experience three dimensions of perception that combine in various ways to give us the realm of colors we see. Like many other animals, we need three types of photoreceptors to make our color vision work. Yet there are some species of animals that use only one dimension of perception. More common are animals that use two dimensions of perception: squirrels, rabbits, deep water fishes, and certain monkeys, for instance. And, amazingly, there are some animals, such as pigeons and goldfish, that use one *more* dimension than we do, that is, a combination of four types of photoreceptors. There may even be species that use five types of photoreceptors, but this has not yet been verified.

We may wonder what different, or extra, colors pigeons and goldfish or other four-dimensionally-sighted animals see that we do not. This is an honest and reasonable enough question but beside the point. Animals seeing in four dimensions, that is, with tetrachromatic vision, do not see better than humans with trichromatic vision. Rather, they see life in a fourth dimension that we cannot presently conceive. It is a totally *different* way of seeing.[1]

This difference in vision stems from the needs of the organism in a complex world. We humans do not *need* to process another dimension of vision for our well-being. Two-dimensionally- sighted deep water fishes, on the other hand, have very different needs in their dark world, as do four-dimensionally-sighted shallow water fishes who must know the difference between blue sky, blue water, and blue fish. A four-dimensionally-sighted pigeon is not more evolved because it has one more dimension of seeing than the human being. It simply has different needs. The number of dimensions is not a matter of hierarchy, of one being better than another —a tendency in the Newtonian worldview—but of relationship between the environment and the creature's needs. "Need" is central to paradigm shifting. A paradigm shift is a matter of adding a new dimension of understanding to our lives because we *need* it.

What is heart-breaking about the paradigm-shifting process is that people tend to believe that the values they hear expounded by the new worldview—ecological concerns, for instance—can simply be incorporated into the Newtonian worldview. This would be like putting four-dimensional vision into an animal that has only three-dimensional faculties. A paradigm shift is not a matter of fine-tuning what we already use, or even seeing it in greater detail. Instead, an entirely new dimension(s) emerges to show us that the world is very different from what we had previously envisioned.

It is important to note, however, that a paradigm shift does not negate what has gone before. Usually, when we obtain more up-to-date information, our first tendency is to toss aside what has been taught before. But a paradigm shift does not mean we throw the baby out with the bath water. Former scientific knowledge, for example, is not so much incorrect as inadequate. Previous knowledge *can* be saved and used, but as physicist Thomas Kuhn points out, its domain of application becomes more restricted.[2]

A simple illustration of this concept can be seen in the development of maps. For all intents and purposes, two-dimensional maps worked well for the explorers of the fifteenth century. Coordinates on a flat map allowed people to go to places they had never been before or to return to them exactly. This information and understanding worked fine, based on the premises that the world was flat and that the earth was the center of the universe.

There came a day when the need and desire for expansion —to know more, to see more—ran up against fear: the fear of falling off the end of the world. Finally, someone dared to observe that the earth must be round. Though the flat map might have been accurate on the local level, at a certain point of scale, a leap in understanding of the earth as a globe rather than as a flat plane was necessitated. Thus the world's understanding of itself took a dramatic shift, a paradigm shift. We still use flat maps. They are most helpful. We have lost the sea monsters on the edges, however.

There seems to come a point when need overrides fear. For instance, as long as we did not need to travel around the world, or into outer space, we did not need anything beyond a flat road map. Or, as long as we felt there was plenty of space on the earth, we had no trouble throwing trash away. But now that there is hardly any space left into which to toss our things, we are having to learn to value items more for their relationship to the environment than for any intrinsic value of the individual entities themselves.[3] As a result, we have created entire catalogs of environmentally-friendly products available in bulk or recyclable containers. The world has changed, and so have our needs.

Even though paradigm shifts are driven by need, they still do not come easily for us. There is a great grinding of gears. On that long-ago night after hearing Anne Wilson Schaef, I was so excited that I ran right into the classroom with my new insights. I was eager, exuberant, and naïve. I offered experiments in exegesis in the classroom. I wrote "alternative" papers. I maintained my grade point as a first-year student in classes usually reserved for second- and third-year students. One morning I was told by one of the leading professors at this institution that if I intended to challenge him in the classroom, as I had other professors, I would no longer be welcome to enroll in his classes. For the first time I realized that a line had been drawn—by them, not me. Either my work was valid and their Ph.D.'s were not, or my work was invalid and their Ph.D.'s were. I left academia at the end of that year.

I did not set up a dichotomy of either "they're right" and "I'm wrong," or "I'm right" and "they're wrong." I did not see it that way at all. I just saw the context and domain of their work differently. For the first time in my study of religion, my theology had emerged in living color.

Prior to this shift, when I had been studying the theologians of the times, such as Kierkegaard or Kant or Tillich or Bultmann, my mind would become like a black-and-white television screen, "either/or" in orientation, and I would feel sterile, unimaginative, and arid. I perceived that Western theology had hit a brick wall years ago, and we were still wandering back and forth along the length of that same old wall pretending we were getting somewhere. Every new bit of theology I encountered seemed to be a variation on the same theme, a theme that was killing my own colorful spirit. I needed more. I had grown restless as a student of theology. I knew that somehow there needed to be a new way of seeing, and though I was as capable as the next person of wandering eloquently along that old wall, I could not get excited about the standard theology. The night I heard Anne Wilson Schaef, I realized that these German theologians represented only one tangent in an entire circle of possible tangents of understanding. This did not negate their valuable contributions but rather acknowledged that much was missing.

I attended a high-powered "think tank" sponsored by the Berkana Institute on the new sciences and leadership. This particular inquiry involved leadership and self-organizing systems.[4] The participants were corporate and government management consultants from across the country. One very conservative-looking man, raised in the Midwest and a lifelong bureaucrat in Washington, D.C., said in the closing session:

> At work, a few of us in management refer to ourselves as BWB's. Do you know what that means? "Boring white boys." Now, don't get me wrong. I liked my life, and I'm not putting myself down, but I know I've missed out on a lot because of it. I lost a sense of meaning somewhere. It's one of the reasons I came here.[5]

Here was a high-ranking manager in one of Washington's departments, a good man, who sensed that there was more to life than what he had previously understood. Rather than feel frightened and threatened by what he sensed, however, he had decided to dance the uncertainty and venture into unknown territory such as this conference. He had done nothing "wrong" and was a success by hierarchichal Newtonian standards, and yet he knew on some level that there was more to be had, another dimension of life to be lived. Paradoxically, the very worldview that had given him (not to mention Western civilization) its greatest achievements (and some very great things they are) was now leading to his (and our) demise.

Paradoxes are disconcerting to most people, yet awareness of paradox is crucial to understanding a paradigm shift because paradoxes are the *precursors* of paradigm shift. In simplest terms, paradox is the apparent presentation of contradictory truths. This can be expressed mathematically, for instance: Picture an equation where A does not equal B ($A \neq B$). Either A or B can be true but not both of them. If A is true, then we would assume that B is not true and vice versa. If, however, it appears that *both* A and B are true, then there is a paradox.

Some paradoxes are simpler than others. Two waves of sound, for example, can meet each other in such a way as to cancel one another out. Where there were originally two sounds, there is now silence. This phenomenon is known as *destructive interference.*[6]

Our universe is full of paradoxes. Take, for instance, a vacuum, which we tend to think of as empty space, void of anything we value. Yet, paradoxically, a vacuum is the very condition most likely to create matter. What we imagine to be still and empty is actually full of the tendency toward disorderliness. The second law of thermodynamics teaches us that a body naturally tends toward disorder, randomness, to assuming as many different states as it can. This is the concept of *entropy.*[7]

At the same time, *quantum fluctuation* occurs in the vacuum of outer space. Quantum fluctuation creates the probability that conditions will collide or intersect over a matter of time in the void until there is an eruption of energy exchange. The "big bang" theory postulates that the beginning of the cosmos may have been the result of just such a quantum fluctuation within the void.[8] The paradox of a vacuum is actually quite exquisite: What we commonly perceive as empty is inevitably bound to conceive. In some ways a vacuum is the consummate womb.

A current crucial paradox involves the root understanding of the universe, a paradox that Einstein himself could not reconcile. On one hand, there is a general theory of relativity, which NASA uses successfully on the global level. This theory describes the force of gravity and the large-scale structure of the universe. On the other hand, there is the theory of quantum mechanics dealing with phenomena on extremely small scales, which nuclear physicists use quite successfully in the subatomic realm. Yet these two theories "are known to be inconsistent with each other—*they cannot both be correct*."[9] It is enough to drive any scientist crazy. It is ironic that science carries the prestige it does in the face of this gaping paradox.

Yet another paradox involves Einstein's great theory, $E=mc^2$. While billions of stars burn in hundreds of thousand millions of galaxies—more than we can even begin to imagine—the sum total of the energy of the universe is zero.[10] Energy is never lost unless matter is gained, and matter is never gained unless energy is lost.

Then there is the paradox of information. "Information," for most of us, generally means an awareness of some fact that we had not known before. We tend to think of information as something that is *added* to our knowledge bank. Science, however, is discovering "information" is not that which is added, but that which *differentiates*.[11] Even our bodies understand this. As human beings, we are receptors of such incredible amounts of stimuli that we block out most of it to survive. Our bodies constantly produce inhibitory feedback to suppress the overload of stimuli.[12]

I came to understand this concept of differentiation first-hand when I traveled to Japan. I had heard that the Japanese culture was very cooperative, in contrast to the individualistic American culture. This information was lodged in my head along with a million other tidbits, but it meant nothing to me, really, until it became a personal experience. When yet one more Japanese woman told me how to wash my clothes in the washing machine, to the extent of delineating the exact order of placement of each piece of clothing in the machine, I began experiencing an extreme case of "I'll do it my way—I don't care what anyone else says." Then came the day when I walked by a small home being roofed by twelve Japanese carpenters doing the task together. I realized that twelve carpenters in America would probably *kill* each other before they could get on one tiny roof and work together like that. Once I had this context, this boundary of experience in which to put things together, I then had the capacity to differentiate the words "co-operative" and "individualistic" in ways I had never conceived before.

At the point we are able to see difference, to differentiate, to distinguish between things, we come to awareness. This awareness of differentiation IS information. Information is what we see *in contrast*. Information is the result of recognizing boundaries, or of circumscribing.

For me, perhaps the most exciting paradox comes from the new biology discovery that the first cell did not appear until indistinguishable bacteria joined together in relationships, limited their interactions, and emerged into a single cell. What this tells us is that, in the "prokaryotic world (i.e., all life until a mere 1.2 billion years ago) *nothing smaller than a community can be an individual.*"[13] That is a very revolutionary paradox!

Perhaps equally transforming is the paradox of death. "For billions of years, death was not a biological necessity. . . . "[14] However, as life-forms became more complex and increased in number, the invention of death appeared. Think of it: Without death, we would be surrounded in garbage from the beginning of time. There would be now no room for the creative movement of life-forms. We would not have had the opportunity to develop systems that embrace simpler organisms: tissues from cells, organs from tissues, bodies from organs, etc.

Clearly, paradox is at the root of the new sciences and the new worldview they present. All of these paradoxes defy what we know as "common sense." There are many more. Our very way of thinking is paradoxical in and of itself. We are comforted by "order" while at the same time being fascinated by the prospect of unlimited possibility. Perhaps that is why chaos is one of the most popular paradoxes today: Chaos exhibits order yet is infinite possibility; it is contained and yet is unlimited.[15] The very awareness of this plethora of paradoxes is a signpost of an impending paradigm shift, or shift of worldview.

Yet we are not comfortable with either paradoxes or paradigm shifts. If two things are not equal, it is easier to think that only one can be true, not both, UNLESS . . . there is a greater truth that embraces both of them. And therein lies the central gift of paradox: With greater truth comes greater understanding, an understanding that had previously seemed impossible.

But most of us have trouble believing or trusting that a "greater truth" will emerge. We have been well programmed to think that what we know now—especially in the sciences—has been the result of a smooth progression of accurate, precise, detailed, and verifiable information. In reality, there have been thousands of experiments that have led nowhere, or were in error, even misleading. Often experiments do not build on former experiments. We choose which facts to record historically, and which not. For example, the "father" of modern Western science, Isaac Newton, also had a deep belief in God, not to mention astrology and alchemy,[16] information that we seldom read or hear about. Science has never been as orderly, as pure, or as clear as history tends to portray it.

However, we are understandably reluctant to give up our entrenched perceptions. No one goes around seeking a paradigm shift unless the present perception of reality is seen to be seriously flawed. The process of relinquishing control, of abandoning familiar ways of doing things, may seem too great a challenge no matter how much acceptance we give, on a cognitive level, toward a new paradigm. The uncertainty that accompanies the actual process of changing a worldview is far from comforting.

Once a new worldview is in place, we sigh with relief and, like children, begin to explore this new world we have discovered. I, for example, am one of those people I refer to good-naturedly as a "techno-peasant." I do not relate easily with technologically advanced devices. I was one of the last of my peers to learn to use a computer. However, once I realized what the computer could do for me, you could not keep me from it.

Many blocks can stand in the way of a new paradigm coming into being: the power dynamics of money, class, politics. Although a new worldview does not negate the contributions of a former worldview, this is a difficult concept for those who fear that their world, heretofore quite successful, may be about to fall apart. Under such conditions a person can easily become reactionary, clenching fists out of frustration and fear.

> Shallow ideas can be assimilated; ideas that require people to reorganize their picture of the world provoke hostility. [17]

We may experience paradigm shifting a bit like having the rug shaken out from under us. Unless we are prepared, it may be a rather earth-shaking experience, especially if we crash to the floor, embarrassed or angry—and probably in pain. We are rarely eager to engage a new worldview. There does come a time, however, when rather than further explore a prevailing worldview, someone becomes convinced that the present worldview is flawed or inadequate and begins to "imagine" a different worldview. This is the point at which problems arise.

The pursuit of knowledge within the current paradigm is known as "normal science." Since our experience of scientists is almost exclusively of those engaged in normal science, we tend to equate all science with normal science.[18] Many scientists are quite content to stay within normal science or the Newtonian worldview.[19] In actuality, normal science is only one facet of science. However, when a scientist leaves the field of what is considered "normal science" for the possibilities of the "new sciences," cries of "kook," "day-dreamer," "waster of time"—not to mention "waster of money"—are heard. After all, who wants to pay anyone to shake up our present worldview?

I am reminded of the treatment of Masanobu Fukuoka, author of *The One-Straw Revolution*.[20] I was privileged to visit Fukuoka's farm in Japan. Though he was in Africa at the time, I spoke at length with one of his students and briefly with his wife. Fukuoka believed there was a different way to farm. He was convinced that farming needed to take into account the interrelatedness between growing things and their environs, and to each other, to such an extent that the *relationships* of the plants would be more important than fertilizer, hybrid seed, or cultivation. He developed a method of farming more closely resembling the way plants tend to grow in their natural environs, acknowledging that certain plants grow better in combination with other plants than they do with others of their own species.

The neighbors and the government of Japan were so upset with this small farmer's scientific experiments arising from a different worldview that they banned international students at his farm. The neighbors deliberately oversprayed his fields with pesticides. Fukuoka was world-famous by this time but had become a *persona non grata* in his own country. In fact, the fight to keep his farm operation in Japan alive has grown to be too much, and Fukuoka is spending his time traveling the world, teaching those who are receptive.

Those who do not have faith that an emerging new paradigm will bring a "greater truth," or who cannot imagine it, perceive only that their worldview is being threatened. They tend to accept only information that supports the prevailing worldview. What happens then, of course, is that the prevailing worldview becomes self-perpetuating. The inherent danger in this cycle is that the denial of information could lead to the extinction of our species.

The role of denial, often in the form of minimalization, is the biggest problem facing us when it comes to a change of worldview. As a society, we have articulated the role of minimalization in addiction. An alcoholic, for instance, may deny the severity of her addiction by stating she only has "a couple of beers" every night, when in reality she has a six-pack. She minimizes the degree of addiction in order to deny its impact on her life.

Facing a change of worldview, a paradigm shift, is as difficult for us as it is for an alcoholic to face his or her addiction. We must be able to acknowledge the seriousness of the problem before we can move forward in resolving it. Many of us are simply overwhelmed. Rather than deal with the paradox that the most powerful nation on earth is in dire trouble, we blindly cling to a worldview that worked once and engage in a severe case of wishful thinking. A simple example is that there are still people who cannot fathom that consuming as little as two drinks and driving, or smoking in confined space, is such a "big deal" today, despite the statistics that point out otherwise.

It is scary to change worldviews. The paradox is that it is equally scary to remain trapped in the present worldview. This was as true at the inception of Western civilization as it is today. Western civilization points to the "Golden Age" of Greece, five hundred years before the birth of Jesus, as its origin. When the Pythagorean community of this ancient Greece discovered what it thought was information incompatible with its worldview—a worldview based on mathematics—at least one member committed suicide, and the entire community dissolved. They could not contain the paradox even for a short while.[21]

Two thousand five hundred years later, the small-farm crisis of the 1980s in the United States provides a similar example. The West was won through the propagation of the theory of rugged individualism. Farmers thrived on this concept. As long as America believed the world was built of isolatable, individual building blocks, it was easy to advance the theory of rugged individualism. This concept, however, worked to the farmer's detriment during the 1980s. Many small farmers were unable to come together to help one another because they saw themselves, within the Newtonian mindset or worldview, as isolated failures. They could not see the web of factors, many beyond their control, that contributed to their demise. If a farmer could not stand on his or her own two feet, it was deemed unnatural. In Missouri in one year alone, thirty-nine farmers put guns to their heads and committed suicide, convinced their failure was their fault alone.

But what if, like the first cells in the billion-year-old prokaryotic world, rugged individualism is *not* natural to the universe? What if the building of community is? Then new possibilities arise. If the farmers had been able to see themselves as integral members of a mutually beneficial commitment, as part of a greater interdependent community rather than as isolated entities, thirty-nine more of them would most likely still be living today.

Despite the fear, denial, individualism, and isolationism, change is happening. Fourteen years after leaving seminary, I visited another seminary class in biblical studies, and there before my very eyes discovered that the type of study I had tried to initiate in the classroom fourteen years before was now a part of the curricula. What I had experimented with then was being taught now. In fact, an entire interdisciplinary department had been established to dance the paradoxes of race and class and gender issues. While it was not a painless realization, it was one of relief.

Arthur Zajonc, a physicist committed to a prophetic vision, has stated:

> If we would create the capacities for understanding our future, then we must *dwell* precisely in the tensions, the paradoxes, the annoying anomalies of our time.[22]

We dare not minimize, avoid, cover over, or anesthetize ourselves.

> On nearly every front we are being called on to
> re-imagine the world we inhabit. It simply awaits an
> act of courage for us to begin, and patient persever-
> ance for us to succeed in the self-conscious educa-
> tion now in our hands.[23]

We must gather the courage and patience to persevere in learning
the Cloudhand—a pattern of endless possibilities—for the chaos
of our times.

ON

WHOSE

AUTHORITY?

I will never forget the time I first saw a 3-D computer image that contained a hidden image invisible on the initial observation. My physicist friend took me to Harvard Square and ushered me into a gallery section of the Coop store. As I stared at the image before me, all I could see was a picture filled with the same repetitive design. When I was finally able to relax my focus, a three-dimensional galactic scene of Pegasus flying around Saturn emerged. As the new image appeared, my eyes filled with tears, and I was overwhelmed with a sense of new meaning: "What has remained hidden can now be seen."[1] For me, these three-dimensional images became a metaphor for hope.

The "trick" to seeing in three dimensions is to stop focusing on obvious detail and relax to a point where you can recognize a difference in depth of field. This is usually accomplished either by trying to look through the picture or by holding the picture right up against your eyes until you are practically cross-eyed and then slowly withdrawing it.

Some of the other people in the gallery with me could not find the image because they could not see the difference in depth of field. This did not make them "wrong"; they simply were not seeing all that they could possibly see. Moreover, there was no way for them to know whether I or anyone else was "making up" what we professed to see. Those who could not see the three dimensions had to judge those of us who did by whether they *believed* we were speaking our own truth or "putting them on." They had to judge our sense of authority.

We are faced with a similar dilemma: Will we see all that we can see? On whose authority can we depend? How will we judge the validity of a new paradigm if the only criteria we have is articulated within the context of a waning worldview? No matter how much knowledge we have proven to be true in the Newtonian paradigm, we have yet to prove *how* we know what we know. Until more recently the study of "how we know," or epistemology, primarily involved rational, logical, philosophical, and theoretical discourse—not necessarily actual experience, and certainly not anything as nebulous as intuition, fantasy, or imagination.

During my recent campaign for public office, I went around and met with department heads in our local county government. I often asked them if they had sufficient information with which to make decisions. They would look at me rather strangely, point to stacks of papers, and respond that they were overwhelmed with information. During this same time, I attended an amazing conference on the new sciences and corporate management where I was encouraged to offer employees even more information. I said that my experience was that people were already inundated with information. A consultant begged to differ with me.

She had recently interviewed employees at a DuPont plant that was operating under several of the principles of the new sciences. She said she watched waves of information flow accurately through the plant on a regular basis. When she asked the employees how they dealt with so much information, they matter-of-factly commented that they were used to it. What was different from their past ways of dealing with information was that each employee was now responsible for deciding which information was useful to them. The decision was no longer relegated only to management.

"But how," asked the consultant, "do you know you choose the right information you need?" The employees responded that they scanned reams of information, but they knew they had found what they needed *when the information resonated with a deeper sense of meaning in their work.* The criteria these employees used for whether or not they had the right information was based on their experiencing meaningfulness, not logic. And this was not a New Age plant distributing crystals, but a chemical plant doing very well, not only among its employees and stockholders, but within its local community![2]

The Newtonian worldview uses a very different criterion for deciding what information is right. Newtonian science, or "normal science," uses the method of *praxis*, that is, the practical application or practice of a theory.[3] A scientific truth, or more accurately a scientific *theory*, may be in use for years with the very real possibility that it may be inaccurate. Scientific truth is merely a theory that has not yet been *dis*proved. In fact, it is not unusual for scientific information to be used with no understanding at all. For example, we invented the light bulb, the telephone, and a hydroelectric plant nine years before anyone had even verbalized the concept of the electron, the theory explaining these inventions.[4]

This is a more fragile way of perceiving scientific truth than what has been commonly understood. In normal science, at the very moment a scientific theory is disproved, all is lost. A good theory is not one that works a majority of the time, or even two-thirds of the time; a good scientific theory must *always* work.

The "underdetermination of theory" presents an even further dilemma. "Briefly stated it reminds us that a finite body of data can certainly be accounted for by more than one theory. How, then, can any one theory provide a uniquely 'true' account of the world?"[5] This is why circumstantial evidence is not acceptable for determining guilt or innocence in criminal trials. More than one scenario can result in the same conclusion. More than one logical series of events can account for the same crime. The trick is to determine the actual one.

Science faces yet another limit: It can only test for what we think we know, at least to a certain point of practicality. But is science, as one systems analyst told me, only the act of reporting accurately what we observe? This has been its claim.

> The sciences do not try to explain, they hardly even
> try to interpret, they mainly make models. By a
> model is meant a mathematical construct.[6]

By this definition, science is the art of observing how and where the world resembles mathematical models. According to Philipp Frank, author of *Philosophy of Science*, science has accepted a few facts, and from them derived a series of logical interpretations and ramifications.[7] "The resulting theoretical system is . . . self-validating and its truth is essentially independent of the physical occurrences in the world."[8] In short, all the scientific theories in the world may be logical, but all are not necessarily accurate. There may be other more adequate and accurate explanations for perceived events.

"Normal science" is a matter of logically extending what is already known. Such a view of science fits neatly into the Newtonian worldview—in fact, is demanded by it. However, physicist Thomas Kuhn asserts that significant scientific discovery of a *paradigm-breaking* nature does not happen within the realm of this "normal science."[9] Paradigm-breaking science happens when a scientists takes time to "imagine" a new way of understanding.

I am not a mathematician and do not envision the universe via numbers. Nor do I believe that mathematical constructs provide a particularly accurate understanding of the universe. Thus, during the course of writing this book, I had to attempt to "imagine" what the scientists with their numbers are saying in a way that is comprehensible to a mind, such as mine, that thinks in images. For instance, in trying to understand the explanation that the "big bang" origin of the universe was the result of a quantum fluctuation, I imagined "quantum fluctuation" as a facial tic. That led me to the word "tick," meaning "beat," and I immediately associated "beat" with "heartbeat." I then wondered if perhaps it might be appropriate to say that the universe was born out of a heartbeat of God.

This thinking process that led me from quantum fluctuation to heartbeat is what Carl Jung called "amplification," or word association. I wonder how much of our attempt to present logical thought is amplified, if not changed subconsciously, by the unexpected appearance of words that send our minds free-associating to an even more accurate portrayal.

Again the problem: How can we know a new paradigm if our criteria for knowing is defined by the logic of the prevailing paradigm? To put it even more simply, how can we live a new way if all we know is the old way?

How does a scientist, who takes time to imagine, know when she has discovered a new theory of significance? Since it cannot be a matter of logic, is it a matter of luck, of the odds winning out? Those are pretty great odds since so few scientists do engage in the type of behavior necessary to paradigm-breaking science. Normal science is such *satisfying* work. It is measurable and clear-cut. Paradigm-breaking science is unnerving because so much of it is unclear, unknown, and there are no models or standards against which to gauge progress. This awareness makes us appreciate even more the few scientists, such as Einstein, who dare to take this journey into the unknown, uncharted territory.[10]

How does an Einstein, or anyone who seems to have glimpsed a new paradigm, *know* that he or she has done so? What is the nature of this recognition? For the person within the old paradigm, *the only way to comprehend the new paradigm initially may be by metaphor*, i.e., the new paradigm is "like . . . " or the paradigm is "as if . . . " We need to use our imagination, which, as Einstein observed, is more important than knowledge.

What gives the discoverers of a new paradigm the courage to assert, at great risk to their credibility if not their lives, that the new discovery is true? What led Columbus to risk running into monsters and falling off the edge of a flat world? What has led scientists to take their own newly discovered vaccines and risk working with contagious patients? This, I would assert, is a profound faith event of the highest order, a spiritual experience, a moment of resonance with a deeper sense of meaning.

After reading a few articles on the new sciences, I noticed that several physicists quoted the nineteenth-century German philosopher, scientist, and *artist* Goethe. I picked up the phone and called one of the physicists and asked if they were all reading the same book or article on Goethe or if this was a spontaneous event. The physics professor responded with, "Who else is reading Goethe?" It seemed to be a serendipitous event. This piqued my interest to find out why present day scientists were resonating with Goethe.

Goethe, a Romantic himself, believed that knowledge is not a matter of adding objects to the brain's knowledge bank. He understood knowledge as an *event*. According to his "cognitive phenomenalism,"[11] we can go through life perceiving or observing many phenomena while having no understanding of these observations, just as many a math student does math problems without the least conceptual understanding of what she is doing. Goethe called this type of knowledge that is simply a matter of facts *"verstand,"* or "discursive analysis," the ability to do logical, rational tasks.[12]

I used to drive my high school algebra teacher crazy, though he maintained a fondness for me anyway. He would place a problem on the blackboard and start explaining it to the class. I was one of those students who really wanted to understand but was not particularly adept at it. After he had finished his explanation, he would mutter, "You get it?," but his eraser was already poised to erase the problem, assuming that of course we did "get it," due to his excellent explanation.

I would thrust my hand into the air in near-panic saying, "Wait a minute!," and this dear teacher would faithfully call on me, waiting with his eraser still poised.

"Yes, Rhea?"

I would then invariably respond, "Oh, I get it!" In just that little lapse of time my brain would have caught up with the class. I justly earned the nickname of "Wait-a-Minute, Oh-I-Get-It!"

Goethe named that "I-got-it" moment the moment of conception. This type of "knowledge-event" depends not only on perceiving the data, but on conceiving the theory behind it, on joining the precept and concept, on observing data and then further seeing how this data relates to an overall theory. Goethe called this understanding of the *relationship* of facts *"vernunft."* Unlike a *verstand* approach of memorizing facts, this approach to knowledge is an "intuitive, or synthetic mode of reasoning."[13]

Another way of understanding the difference between *verstand* and *vernunft* is to think of how people cook. There are some people who cook only by following recipes. This approach to cooking means that a person *cannot* cook without a recipe, without a list of exact items or measurements. This is cooking by *verstand*, by memorizing and accomplishing stated details. There is no discovery or creativity to this approach, no resonance with a greater understanding.

My junior high school home economics teacher tried to teach me to cook in this way, and I found it dull. I took no interest in cooking. Off and on for over twenty years, however, I have worked in restaurants as a cook to subsidize my other work. I have learned to cook another way—by observing the relationships of certain combinations of food and the relationship of certain spices to certain foods. I gained an understanding of food relationships that allowed me to enter a restaurant "walk-in" refrigerator in the morning and, by dinner, generate a delicious meal without the need of predefined recipes or ingredients. I have known some great chefs who put some very creative names on delicious food that is what you or I at home would call leftovers. Rather than trying to find what fits into a preconceived set of recipes, these chefs imagine or conceive concoctions for the evening menu. This is cooking by *vernunft*.

Fortunately, we humans are not merely manipulators of ingredients—or data or information. We are capable of creating innovative meals from what is available, of conception.

What determines that moment of conception? Why is it that some people watch a *t'ai chi* master and yawn, while others discover cosmic truth? What determines, out of an entire classroom of students, whose faces will light up with understanding of the concepts presented? A teacher can "re-present" the data, the observable material at hand, but cannot guarantee a "knowledge-event."[14] Many of us can learn the dance steps, but not all of us will let go enough to experience the conception or art of the dance behind the steps.

Einstein would have described the moment of conception, that "Aha!" moment, as a time when the imagination succeeded. The twentieth-century mathematician Benoit Mandelbrot understood it as the moment of intuition.[15] Philipp Frank also believed that true knowledge, conception, and understanding comes from immediate intuition and imagination, not from analytical or logical thought.[16]

This knowledge-event, this moment of intuition, resembles a mystical event, if we define mysticism as

> ... the type of religion which puts the emphasis on immediate awareness of relation with God, on direct and intimate consciousness of the Divine Presence. It is religion in its most acute, intense and living state.[17]

If a knowledge-event is seen as an "immediate awareness" of knowledge "in its most acute, intense and living state," it would then seem that science and mysticism have much in common. Indeed, Goethe felt that only *vernunft* was capable of touching the Divine.[18]

The "Aha!" moment takes us from not knowing, from a sense of being lost, to a sense of knowing with conviction. Whether we would want it to or not, such an experience leaves us with a sense of faith in our discovery.

Just as a "knowledge-event," or paradigm-breaking science, transcends normal science, so does mysticism transcend dogmatic religious practice or doctrine. We have all met priests, ministers, and believers who practice religion by recipe, so to speak. They may not necessarily resonate with a deeper meaning or spirituality. As well, there are many people who hold worldviews neither Western nor affluent, not dependent on Goethe or Barth or Bultmann, who experience their faith profoundly.

This is true for science as well. In fact, it may be precisely within those cultures that are not as bound to the exploiting of facts, to the logical extension of certain basic assertions, that there lies the freedom and faith to "imagine" breakthroughs in understanding.

As early as 1919, A.M. Beede, a missionary on the Standing Rock Sioux reservation in North Dakota, noticed that scientific thought was not difficult for Indians:

> There is no difficulty in leading an old Teton Sioux
> Indian to understand the 'scientific' attitude. . . .
> The idea of atoms and electrons is easy and pleasing
> to an old Indian, and he grasps the idea of chemistry.
> Such things make ready contact with his previous
> observation and thinking . . . [19]

> But Rising Sun, speaking the conclusion of all, pro-
> nounced the 'scientific view' inadequate. *Not bad,
> or untrue, but inadequate . . .* [20]

Although the Indian culture could follow the details of the
scientific paradigm presented to them, they conceived of a different
worldview that better accommodated the facts of their lives. Annie
Dillard relates the well-worn story of the Eskimo speaking to a
Christian priest. The Eskimo asked the priest,

> "If I did not know about God and sin, would I go to
> hell?"

> "No," said the priest, "not if you did not know."

> "Then why," asked the Eskimo earnestly, "did you
> tell me?" [21]

The priest was attempting to follow the recipe of his faith
from his worldview that was vastly different from that of the
Eskimo. His worldview used the stories of Adam and Eve, and a
place called hell, to explain good and evil in the world and to
encourage people to seek the path of the good. The Eskimo people
derived their worldview from their community's experience in
relationship to a land, climate, and culture vastly different from
that originating in biblical Mesopotamia, the home of the Jewish/
Christian heritage. By the priest's inability to see that his story was
only one vehicle, one recipe, for conveying the truth—rather than
being the truth itself—the priest negated the faith journey of the
Eskimo.

If in our zealousness to communicate *our* worldview, we
assume that the mere memorization or observation of data constitutes understanding or realization, we commit idolatry. *Idolatry is
when we take something for granted and make it holy, whether in*

science or religion, instead of experiencing it for ourselves.

When I was fourteen, I took a field trip with other young people from my denomination to an urban congregation on the south side of Chicago. During the course of a discussion at the church, one of the local leaders severely criticized churches for their refusal to deal with the real problems of the world. He accused the church of being a comfortable place to fulfill social obligations, rather than a place that did Jesus' bidding in the world.

I leapt to my feet and asserted that my church was a very good church indeed. (You need to understand that my father was a minister, and all the churches I had known were those led by my father.) I was furious at his allegations. In my eyes, the church could do no wrong. For me, church was holy. I idolized church. I could not distinguish a particular church from the *concept* of a greater Church. I could not hear the validity of much of his criticism, nor the pain that engendered it because, in my eyes, the church was above criticism. I remember the looks other people in the room gave me after I had spoken, especially the people of color, and I became painfully aware of my own defensiveness. I sat down and from that moment on began to really listen. That day I grasped an entirely new understanding of Church, one that resonated in a much deeper way in my being. I had substituted the activity of my particular church, and any church for that matter, for the actual experience of a deeper meaning of Church in the world.

Scientists do much the same thing when they substitute "re-presentation" for the genuine knowledge-event. Like a religious symbol, a scientific representation, such as a model depicting atoms and molecules, only reminds us of the original event.

> The religious idolater thinks the stone statue of Baal is divinity itself; the materialistic idolater thinks the set of sensor-response-interpreted-as-quark is really the matter, 'the real thing.'[22]

When we rely on a symbol rather than our own experience, then we have fallen into idolatry.[23]

"Normal science." "Normal education." "Normal religion." Each has its place, determined by the needs of a culture. Unfortunately, those who wish to maintain control or orderliness or power may short-circuit the process of people experiencing their own knowing—whether in science or education or religion—by demanding unquestioning obedience to normal science, education, or religion. People with external, vested power, that is, "power-over," such as law enforcement officers, soldiers, university professors, or priests, can use this power as a means of enforcing a precept, an observation, a practice without understanding. It is an easy temptation for those with vested power to become complacent rather than seek the authority that arises out of their own collective and individual experiences. This, too, is the practice of idolatry.

On the other hand, there are times when we encounter "authority," that is, someone who experiences a knowledge-event, who exudes an inner outpouring of conviction, an understanding of relationships that is not externally bestowed but internally conceived. It is possible for soldiers, law enforcement officers, university professors, or priests to carry such authority *if* they have that internal resonance or awakening of understanding.

I never intended to become a religion major in college. I thought I would major in sociology or English. However, one professor who spoke with conviction, and who lived his life in a way that coincided well with his convictions, attracted my attention. I knew I needed to study with this professor, whose specialty was theology. After two years of study, I remember being amazed to discover that he was only 5'1", much shorter than my 5'10". Contrary to his actual size, in my eyes he was a giant, a man of great stature. He was a person of great authority.

The authority that comes from the experiences of a knowledge-event is threatening to those who have been doing very well in the "normal" realm of vested authority. Yet we are attracted to people who speak with this inner authority.

One of history's best kept secrets is that mystics are reformers, if not outright revolutionaries, precisely *because* of their authority. Contrary to public opinion, mystics are not wimpy, hidden away, uninvolved, "other worldly" folk. Mystics experience a vision, a new way of seeing; they believe in these visions and act upon them. Mystics exude authority. Mystics quite regularly shake up worldviews.

St. Francis of Assisi, for example, was so threatening to the ecclesiastical powers-that-be that he had a difficult time obtaining permission to live his vision. Yet the result of his vision was vast education of the ordinary masses of people. St. Teresa D'Avila was an expert at empowerment of women, cleverly bringing insight to her sisters in the convents despite the watchful and critical eyes of the Inquisition.[24] Mahatma Gandhi spent years at a time waiting on God, waiting for the "Aha!" moment to occur when he would try once again to turn the world around. Ernesto Cardenal, twentieth-century mystic and author of the *Cántico Cósmico*, fostered a revolution in Nicaragua. Martin Luther King, Jr.'s memorial testified to the cause of his death: "They said one to another. Behold, here cometh the dreamer. Let us slay him. And we shall see what will become of his dreams."[25]

The fact of the matter is that the authority, or truth of a knowledge-event or mystical event, is rarely given the opportunity to be verified, due to political agendas. The problem is not that there is no way in which to verify the authority of a knowledge-event or mystical event. The problem is that such events are so threatening that we rarely have the opportunity to examine them before the mystics and their ideas are whisked away, belittled, dismissed, swept under the carpet, or destroyed.

The irony is that the real danger lies not in the true mystical or knowledge-event but in the idolatry. Gestalt therapist Barry Stevens has provocatively asked why, when someone steps out of line, we order them back into line rather than asking them where they are going or what they are seeing. When we stop questioning and assume that what is "re-presented" to us is the truth, without ourselves experiencing its validity or authority, we engage in idolatry.

The knowledge-event threatens all idolatry. Wes Jackson, a Kansas prairie farmer and researcher, asserts that science has become idolatrous in ways that we have taken for granted:

> If Jefferson were alive today and involved in setting
> up a new nation, might he insist as strongly on the
> separation of science and state as he did on the
> separation of church and state? The consequence of

the church-state alliance seems small compared to
the ecological and social consequences of the sci-
ences-state alliance.[26]

Germany has shown the world what the idolatrous side of
external authority can do. The United States in Hiroshima and
Nagasaki showed the world what the idolatrous side of the knowledge-event can do. Jim Jones, with the forced drinking of poison
among his followers in Jonestown—not to mention David Koresh
of Waco, Texas—displayed for the world what the idolatrous side
of religion can do. However, just as we cannot cut off scientific
endeavor to preserve ourselves from the horrible dimensions of
scientific development, we cannot cut ourselves off from spirituality
or the mystical experience to preserve ourselves from the charlatans,
impostors, and pretenders. We dare not muzzle the potential of
creativity out of fear. We need, instead, to learn to recognize true
authority in the midst of the clenched fists. Before we can even begin
to verify the authority of the mystical or knowledge-event, *we must
liberate the possibility.*

On the island where I live, the cost of housing has been
sky-rocketing for years, while the wages have remained among the
lowest in the state. For as many years, the working residents had
been told nothing could be done about it. The common assertion
was that it was impossible to provide housing affordable enough for
people who depended on their island wages to live.

Some very creative and persistent citizens got tired of
hearing the same old story over and over again, and of finding
themselves living in tents, trailers, and shacks. They got together
and formed a community land trust. Through grants, loans, volunteer labor, trainings, community education, and immense effort at
overcoming bureaucratic hurdles, fourteen new homes now stand
that are owned and afforded by local low-wage earners.

The biggest obstacles to the building of these homes were
the social and political pressures against people of low-income. One
islander, who deeply believed the stereotypes about low-income
people, developed a severe case of NIMBY (not-in-my-back-yard).
He attended a speaking engagement that I conducted on behalf of
the community land trust. Afterward, he waited around until I was

alone and then threatened my life should the land neighboring his own ever be used for affordable housing. Nevertheless, in the midst of such clenched fists, this community was able to persevere and liberate possibility.

Rosalie Bertell, a biostatistician, Roman Catholic nun, and author of *No Immediate Danger: Prognosis for a Radioactive Earth*, also liberated possibility.[27] She was once put into my safekeeping for three days. During those few days, she filled my mind with facts concerning the effects of low-level radiation that I found bone-chilling in their horror. I knew I could fairly successfully put this information out of my mind as soon as she left, but her job revolved around the constant awareness of this information. I asked her how she was able to deal with the implications of this. She responded that she prayed, and cried, a lot. She is not able to practice her research in the United Sates because there have been several attempts on her life. She lives and conducts her research in exile.

For one of Rosalie's presentations, we invited workers from the Nevada Test Site. One of the workers began questioning her in a rather hostile manner: "How can you know all these so-called effects of low-level radiation when there is no way to measure low-level radiation?"

She responded that there were ways to measure these effects, but it was not with a little machine measuring rads or rems or millicuries. She agreed with the questioner that this type of measurement is useless and inadequate. She observed that science had become fixated on this means of measurement—conveniently so, she added. She said that we simply needed to look for another way to measure.

And she found one—in the Department of Public Health statistics. By checking the statistics of residents living every mile, two miles, ten miles, twenty miles, sixty miles, etc., downwind or downstream from nuclear reactors or uranium mines who were suffering from cancer, premature infant births and deaths, thyroid problems, etc., she came up with a remarkable standard of measurement.

At the time, Rosalie Bertell was breaking ground in a very hostile environment. She managed to dance the chaos in such a way as to conceive a solution, not by using the content of normal science, but by resonating with the relationships of information she was encountering. Today, the same victims of low-level radiation experimentation are seeking recompense themselves.

We need to find ways of testing the authority of a knowledge-event as creatively and effectively as did Rosalie Bertell. When are we being given a "re-presentation" of reality and when is something the genuine experience of a knowledge-event? Perhaps all too purposely, we are often told there is no way to measure the validity of an experience. We are told that our experiences are too individualistic and subjective, inappropriate for scientific endeavor, which stands outside of moral, ethical, or spiritual concerns.

Like Rosalie, I contend that we just have not yet recognized the appropriate measurement tool. The measurement tool that we need must measure the authority of a knowledge-event or paradigm-breaking understanding, not the details or recipes of our more familiar normal course of events. Prior to using the measurement tool, we must lay the groundwork, define the parameters, frame the context. To lay the groundwork, we need to take into account three factors.

First, we must liberate possibility by identifying the *power issues* at work. Where does the vested authority or power lie in each situation? We need to note in particular what effect some new knowledge or discovery would have on the power of the prevailing paradigm, as well as on the discoverer. For instance, for years women have complained about the methods of birth control offered them by medical researchers who were predominantly male. Often these methods had serious side effects on women. One of the intra-uterine devices (IUDs) of my lifetime was so dangerous that the company who manufactured them was forced to pay multiple damage suits. There were indeed potential rewards for the women—if they had no trouble with their IUDs. But for the manufacturers, there were enormous profits to be made from the sale of the product to as many women as possible. The power factor of money was driving the discovery of the IUD and clearly behind the controversy at hand.

Secondly, we need to determine if the discoverer puts his or her *life on the line* with the discovery. For instance, would the medical researcher use the technique of birth control on himself?

Many women believe that they have had to carry the burden of contraception precisely because male researchers do not want to put themselves through such experimentation. Having to put one's life on the line tends to discourage flights of fancy and verifies the experience as an "Aha!," spoken with conviction.

A third factor demands the willingness of both the prevailing paradigm and the discoverer to *engage their fears*. What is the discoverer afraid will happen if his or her technique is not accepted? In the same way, what are the fears of society if the new technique does become acceptable? These questions help us to see what the issues really are and whether they are relevant.

Fear takes many forms. Carl Jung, a scientist and another avid student of Goethe, spoke of the role of the "shadow," the part of ourselves that we do not like and that we tend to reject. He believed that we fear our "shadow" and tend to repress our fear in our unconscious. The unconscious, he went on to say, influences, if not determines, much of our behavior. For example, the unconscious is the instigator of what Jung called "projection": the act of putting onto others characteristics that are actually issues within ourselves. The bottom line is that we simply do not act on what we rationally think. In fact, we often rationalize our behavior to justify actions that have been instigated by the unconscious. Ultimately, the fear we have repressed in our unconscious becomes prime material to erupt into inappropriate but rationalized external behavior.

One of Jung's students, Erich Neumann, took this information and, out of it, offered a new view of ethics. In his *Depth Psychology and a New Ethic*, he stated that not only does an individual person have a shadow side, but it is possible for a group of people, whether a nation, corporation, family, church, or community, to have an unconscious shadow side as well.[28] Therefore, it is also important to bring into consciousness the shadow of the community, whether scientific or religious. We need to ask ourselves, "What are we afraid of?" Otherwise, we risk fooling ourselves into thinking we control our behavior rationally. An honest look at what we fear most—and what we idolize—will tell us much more about ourselves than about others and will free others from being victims of our projections and shadow sides.

With this groundwork in place, we can bring out the measuring tool. A representative of the prevailing paradigm and the discoverer of the new paradigm are brought before the gathered community. The community is faced with the challenge of deciding whether or not what the discoverer is presenting is valid. Does this person exude inner authority or outside power? The evaluation process consists of the following steps that comprise the measuring tool:

Imagine a group comprised of ordinary people who are committed to being a compassionate society, regardless of ethnicity or gender or race or economic development. They value honesty and forthrightness over political savvy, humility over hubris, openness over rigidity, generosity over self-absorption, and service over self-aggrandizement. In short, the community members are mature enough to face their own fears and not be threatened by, invested in, nor reactionary to a given paradigm. They might be characterized as wise (though not to be confused with learned or intellectual) or perhaps as elders. This community is the decision-making body that operates according to these steps:

1. Each perspective is given a *full hearing*, as long as either party wishes, without interruption. There is the attempt to leave nothing hidden or unsaid. It is particularly important to hear all fears from both perspectives.

2. Each states in their own way their *commitment to the benefit of the community* and agrees to submit to the community's judgment, or disengage from the community.

3. Each has an *advocate speak* on his or her behalf.

4. Each *confesses the shortcoming* of her or his worldview.

5. The gathered community then discusses the matter, perhaps with a significant period of silence, and *submits a judgment*, based not on the content of the experience presented—nor whether the person is right or wrong, but on the authority of the experience being witnessed, on a resonance with a deeper sense of meaning among the members of community.

6. If the authority of the knowledge-event is judged to be genuine, then all resources of the community will be utilized within the context of this new vision, or new worldview, or new paradigm, to aid further clarification and be judged accordingly.[29]

I can imagine there are those from the "hard sciences" who would say that the truth of a knowledge-event cannot be determined by such a group consensus as this. And I would ask in response, "Is this so different from how it is determined today? Are we not kidding ourselves to think that most of so-called scientific decision-making today happens by anything other than the politics of the prevailing paradigm-bound elders?"[30] Until we recognize the politics involved in science, we may be forced to wait until the present paradigm-bound elders die off, as Max Planck suggests, before new paradigms can break through.[31]

The Newtonian worldview would assert that this method of measuring—taking into account the role of fear and its concomitant reactionary behavior, not to mention control and strength of conviction, upon our lives—is naïve. I contend that this method, like any good scientific method, is based on experience. It *would* be naïve to suggest that decision-making is accurately accomplished without taking politics or power into account. It *would* be naïve to think that accuracy could be determined without taking into account the nature of the observer and the observation. It *would* be naïve to think we can determine accuracy and authenticity by a measuring tool independent of human influence. The reality is that whatever measurement tool we use, *we* ordinary human beings wield it. The reality is that knowledge-events have always been a matter of faith, of resonance with a deeper meaning, of the discoverer somehow realizing that she will stake her reputation on the new discovery.

When a community can draw on and trust its own inner resources to discover the validity of a new paradigm, the community is liberated from bondage to old, embedded, fixated ways of being in the world. The community is then able to embrace the creativity of chaos, the possibilities of dreams. People are empowered to imagine new ways of being, to problem-solve on a deep level. In this way a community can truly take hold of its future—and its past. Together, the gathered people can soar with their dreams, weep over their losses, and be free to gather together beyond differences of opinion.

A familiar saying declares that we never step into the same river twice: The content of the water in the river is ever changing. Yet there is a definite entity of river that remains the same for us. What we see as "river," however, is not the individual component parts that comprise it, since moment by moment the water changes, bits of the sides of the bank dissolve, and the depth and width of the river is in constant flux. Rather, what we recognize as "river" is designated by the persisting relationship of the water to the land according to a definite pattern.

A

PARADIGM

OF

PATTERNS

Dr. Deepak Chopra points out a similar phenomenon regarding the human body. Each month our skin replaces itself, each three months our seemingly solid skeleton does the same; the whole body (98%), including the brain, replaces itself over the span of only one year.[1] The actual particle components of the human body are constantly changing, and yet there remains a recognizable entity that we call our body that appears unchanging to us. It is the *pattern of relationships* that those ever-changing particles assume that gives us our sense of body.

Another example of pattern relationships is the girls' volleyball team at our island's high school. Every year the individual players change, and yet there remains a team that is beloved more for its relationship to the game than for its record of win/losses. The team is known for its concentration, passion, attention to group dynamics, and positive attitude.

These examples—the river, the human body, the team—seem like matters of common sense. Yet, when taken to the minuscule level of atomic particles on the one hand, or to the magnitude of galaxies on the other, they illustrate the essential difference between the Newtonian worldview and the new sciences.

The pursuit of particularity of content, of detail, is a signpost of scientists in the Newtonian mindset. The Newtonian mindset studies the river by detailing the quantity and speed of water flow, identifying what is dissolved in the water, daily recording its width and depth, and more. The same mindset views the body by dividing it into its separate parts: bones, blood, cells, genes, DNA—that is, the most minute details of anatomy. Newtonians would approach sports in a similar fashion, by identifying the weight and height of players, how many points a particular player scores, how many runs are batted in, how many errors, and so on. The assumption is that the accumulation of these particular details about the parts is all we need to know to understand the whole.

In the same way, the Newtonian mindset has led scientists to look more deeply at the atom, hoping to find the simplest, distinct, individual building block of existence. This pursuit is known as "reductionism," the process of reducing the world to its individual, component parts. For the reductionist, the whole is merely and literally the sum of its parts. It is a neat and tidy conception of the universe that lends itself well to our desire for control.

This neat and tidy worldview was dealt a major blow by the work of physicist Werner Heisenberg. He discovered that there is no exact measurement,[2] and we have been reeling from that fact ever since. Heisenberg studied the tiniest particles in the universe at the subatomic level. He noticed that if he pinpointed a subatomic particle's *position*, he could not pinpoint the particle's *momentum* because, in so doing, he changed the position of the particle. Likewise, he could pinpoint a particle's *momentum* but he could not then pinpoint its *position* without changing its momentum.[3] This process was as discouraging as trying to pick up a piece of quicksilver by hand. In short, he found that stopping to look at something changed everything.

Heisenberg's discovery, called the "uncertainty principle," demonstrated that there was no way to determine that any particle of matter really exists in a particular place and a particular time. You can imagine that this came as quite a shock to the believers of a building-block type of universe where everything is supposed to have its precise place. This uncertainty principle turned the Newtonian world topsy-turvy.

The Newtonian mindset is obsessed with looking at the component parts, with the details. We have huge, extremely expensive facilities to isolate the activity of one proton, whether in a cyclotron or a facility studying proton decay.[4] With advances in microscopic technology, we have worshipped the Petri-dish experiments.

> "Pure cultures" of bacteria, that is, cultures in Petri dish concentration camps, are just bacteria whose social and community behavior has been reduced to the level that we investigators can manage. *But we miss the point.*[5]

These experiments are very limited in what they can tell us. They can only tell us the results of an ideal situation that is sterile and controlled, whereas reality is chaotic and fertile.

Trying to pinpoint reality is actually more like an act of putting a prism or crystal to light and isolating a color on paper. The prism or crystal bends the direction of the original white bright light and projects it into a specific location where we see the wondrous colors of the rainbow. When we try to look at the component parts of light, we actually change the very nature and location of the beam of light. The new worldview says that particularity is transient, deceiving, and dependent on the where, when, how long, and by whom the observation is done. Because looking at the component parts is the result of *someone or something stopping matter in time and space for a moment for a purpose,* the observer has an enormous role in determining the outcome of what he or she sees in any given experiment.

In effect, the new sciences have destroyed certainty, which had been one of the most comforting aspects of science under the Newtonian worldview. Once this realization sinks in, the Newtonian question of what the essential building blocks of the universe are becomes a very different, more complicated question: "What creates the semblance of solidity, separateness, and individuality in an essentially empty and immaterial universe the true nature of which is indivisible unity?"[6] In other words, what makes our world seem so solid and stable when, in fact, we cannot pick out even one tiny individual piece, floating in enormous distances of empty space, without changing our world in the process?

Go back, for a moment, to the volleyball metaphor. Our island team does win a lot of games, but the scoreboard is not what brings people to those games. Rather, people are attracted by the spirit of the event. Individuals meld into a dance of sheer beauty out on the court floor in the midst of a contest of points. The game brings people together because of an appreciation of art, team spirit, passion—qualities much more nebulous than the ability of individuals to score points.

Like the volleyball team, the universe is comprised of something more nebulous than individual building blocks. If someone takes a snapshot of the game, there is no way that it can capture the reality of the team. We can only see a few of the players in a particular maneuver at a particular moment, but there is no picture that expresses the reality of the team, or of the game.

Just so, when we look at subatomic particles, we condense them into a snapshot of being that is as limited as a snapshot of a game—and as limited as to what it can tell us about the universe. Energy, momentum, and electric charge occur according to rules, but instead of distinguishing the *content* of the particles, these rules determine their *relationships.* This is vastly different from the Newtonian emphasis on "things," on content, on objects, on nouns. The new scientific paradigm focuses on patterns of relationships, on movement, on verbs—on how interconnections take place. "In fact, pattern recognition is at the heart of this new cognitive science."[7]

In volleyball, as in the universe, the interconnections are more important than the content. The coach does not say that player A should respond first, and player C next, etc. Rather, the coach tells the team to wait and see where the ball is placed, and where the opponent is standing, to determine who and how to respond. A good team not only notices the pattern of relationships on its opponent's side, but also the team members enter into relationship with one another and with the game in a way that goes beyond their individual abilities. So, too, does each of us live among many interlocking fields of potential relationships.

Music provides another apt metaphor for the significance of relationship patterns over particulars. All Western music —whether it is country western or rock or classical—employs the same twelve notes of the scale. The difference among types of music is made by the patterns of relationships between the individual notes, via the pitches, rhythm, and tempo, and the ways in which they are repeated.

The same is true of language. Many languages share the same small number of phonetic sounds, but the difference among languages is shaped by the pitch and rhythm of the sounds, and by the patterns of repetition. The individual notes of music and the individual phonetic sounds of language exist only as we use them for a particular purpose at a particular time.

This distinction between "particulars" and "pattern" cannot be emphasized enough. The old worldview valued particularity. The old worldview assumed that if there were no individual building blocks that we could isolate and control, then chaos would prevail. And, since chaos was assumed to be absolute randomness, out-of-control, it was terrifying in its possibilities. Yet, the scientific exploration of chaos is precisely that which has provided the breakthrough for understanding this new paradigm of patterns.

Before the advent of the computer, the study of chaotic mathematical equations had been slowed, if not stymied, by their complexity. With advances in computer technology, even the most complicated of equations can be imaged on a computer screen. One of the first people to do so was the weather researcher Edward

Lorenz. Lorenz noticed that certain chaotic equations followed recognizable patterns. The computer illustrated that chaos contains infinite possibility in that no pathway is ever exactly repeated. But the computer also illustrated that the pathway follows a definite pattern—in this case, a pattern similar to the shape of a butterfly. Chaos turns out to be ordered disorderliness. Its infinite nature is contained in a definite pattern (see Figure 1, page 17).

It has been said that "the chaos Lorenz discovered, with all its unpredictability, was as stable as a marble in a bowl."[8] If you take a marble and roll it in a bowl, it will go around and around, never leaving the bowl, never repeating the same orbit exactly, never coming to the same place twice; and yet it will pursue a definite pattern over and over again.

The paradox of chaos will not be denied. Just as the marble never goes outside of a distinct pattern but also never exactly repeats itself, so too does the *t'ai chi* practitioner of Cloudhand consistently follow the same pattern but never puts her hands or feet in exactly the same spot twice.

I never quite understood this phenomenon, never had that moment of "Aha!," until I saw the work of the English scientist Lewis Richardson and, later, Benoit Mandelbrot.[9] They came upon this insight regarding chaos when studying the problem of measuring coastlines. Generally speaking, the measurement of a coastline varies only according to the exactness of the measuring tool the surveyor uses.

For instance, does the surveyor measure every cove? What about measuring around the boulders of each cove? What about measuring around each and every rock, tree, and plant that defines the coastline? A coastline is clearly contained within a defined space, yet it is infinitely measurable. The measurement of the coastline ultimately depends on the degree of exactness of the measurer and the measuring device.

I live in a county that has more saltwater coastline than any other county in the nation. But no matter how infinitely I measure the coastline of my island, it will always maintain its general shape or pattern, and it will never be larger than the mainland it faces.

Like the pathway of the marble, infinite in possibility yet contained within a pattern, the pathway around the coastline follows a specific pattern. But it, too, is infinite in particular measurement. When these chaotic patterns of infinite possibility are enfolded upon themselves, that is, one pattern inside another *ad infinitum*, this is referred to as the "fractal dimension" of a system.

One simple example of a fractal is broccoli. The pattern of an entire head of broccoli is repeated in each individual floret and part of a floret, no matter how little the floret. A fern is another example of a fractal found in biology. The most popular fractals today, featured on the front of greeting cards and calendars, are computer-generated images of chaotic nonlinear equations or chaos. Broccoli, ferns, computer-generated images—each different yet each sharing the common pattern of being a fractal.

Scientists noticed the fractal pattern when they began to encounter chaotic situations in unrelated fields of meteorology, physics, or biology. As the images on the computer changed, there was always a clearly defined pattern within which nothing was ever exactly repeated.

Mandelbrot helped me even further in understanding fractals. He isolated a set of photographs of a fractal generated by the results of a mathematical equation projected onto a computer screen. These photographs show the fractal at varying points of magnification.[10] What is so fascinating about this "Mandelbrot set" is that the more the detail is magnified, the more one discovers a pattern existing within a pattern, much like the reflection of a mirror within a mirror within a mirror, *ad infinitum*. The complex fractal is an exponential enfolding of the simple pattern of itself within itself (see Figures 3-9, pages 68-69).

This may seem a difficult concept for those of us trained in the Newtonian mindset, but educators are finding that children relate very quickly to the concept of fractals, just as they take naturally to learning new languages.

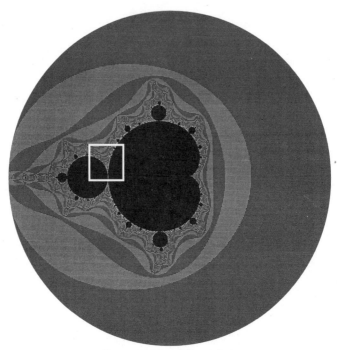

Figure 3. Mandelbrot Set.

Figures 4 – 9 show a magnification of the inset from the preceding figure.

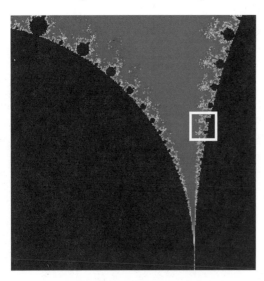

Figure 4. Magnification of inset
from Figure 3.

Figure 5. Magnification of inset
from Figure 4.

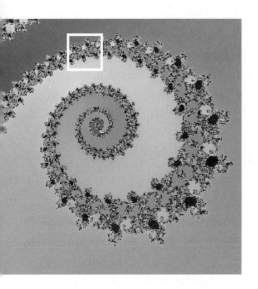

Figure 6. Magnification of inset
from Figure 5.

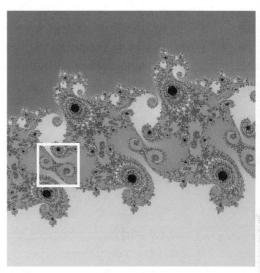

Figure 7. Magnification of inset
from Figure 6.

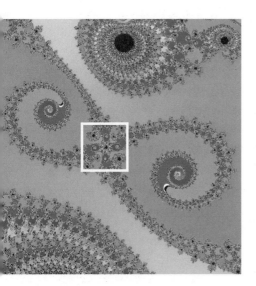

Figure 8. Magnification of inset
from Figure 7.

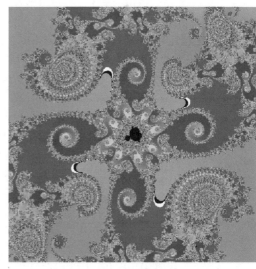

Figure 9. Magnification of inset
from Figure 8.

One professor told of an experience with her five-year-old daughter.[11] The young girl, with whom the professor regularly shared many of the principles of the new sciences, understood and particularly loved fractals. One day the girl's teacher held up a picture of a maple leaf and asked the class what it was. The young girl raised her hand and matter-of-factly answered that it was a fractal. The teacher looked at her sadly and then asked the class again if any of them knew what she had in her hand. After a period of silence, the daughter answered a second time, "It's like broccoli. It's a fractal." The teacher finally told the class that she was holding a picture of a maple leaf.

Later that night the little girl asked her mother, the professor, if a maple leaf was a fractal, and her mother said yes. Both the mother and daughter went about their evening business, when an hour or so later, the mother received a phone call from her daughter's teacher suggesting that the girl be given some psychological and intelligence testing. The mother was taken aback and asked what behavior on her daughter's part had prompted such a request. The teacher responded that her daughter was confusing images such as broccoli and maple leaves!

This professor's daughter had been in danger of being misdiagnosed as ill or disabled because of a difference in worldview. This reaction is not new, but it is distressing and reminds us of the difficulty of trying to operate out of a new mindset.

The concept of fractals has many implications. In fractal theory what is significant are the *patterns* of relating, not what is related. The new sciences have discovered that similar patterns of behavior exist even when the details or content of the participants change. Biologists and their Petri dishes, meteorologists and their weather maps, sociologists and their population studies, and mathematicians and their equations have all discovered that the same patterns work for each of their disciplines—despite the fact that the content of their disciplines differs dramatically.[12]

I am reminded of a time when I was involved in an intervention in the life of an alcoholic near and dear to me. In the course of preparing for that intervention, I learned there were certain patterns under which alcoholics operate, as do their children. The alcoholic denies to those closest in the family unit that there is a problem, that anything is wrong. Meanwhile, the family observes the alcoholic's world continue to narrow in interest and widen in preoccupation with the need for a constant and increasing supply of alcohol. The alcoholic demands that the children collude in the denial of the problem in order to maintain the family secret out in the world. These children often find it very difficult in adult life to maintain intimacy because their formative childhood was based on learning a pattern of behavior that denied reality and kept people away from the truth in their lives. These patterns of behavior exist whether the alcoholic—or child of an alcoholic—is a man or woman, affluent or indigent, upper-class or working-class, white or black, intelligent or ignorant, moral or immoral. And these patterns are hard to break. It is only in the *recognition* of a pattern of behavior that the pattern can be altered.

This idea of "pattern recognition" is key to understanding the new paradigm. Even big business is beginning to take note of the importance of pattern recognition. The Sloan School of Management at Massachusetts Institute of Technology (MIT) contends that the future of corporations lies in their ability to resolve problems by recognizing patterns. Peter Senge, Director of the Systems Thinking and Organizational Learning Program at MIT, has discovered that almost all management problems arising in corporate America stem from less than twenty patterns of structure, or what he calls "systems archetypes." Managers from Ford, Digital, Apple, Procter and Gamble, Royal Dutch/Shell, and others are also studying this pattern phenomena.[13]

The contemporary scientist Stuart Kauffman devised an experiment to illustrate that the universe operates according to orderly sets of patterns. He came up with the premise that there is "order for free" in the universe. He designed a simple exercise on the computer in which he designated ninety light bulbs. Each light bulb was connected to two other light bulbs with the same two sets of instructions.

The instructions were simple and limited, yet the probability or chance of the lights operating in the same way twice, that is, according to the same pattern, was 10 to the 30th power, a phenomenal number beyond our imagination. To understand 10 to the 30th power, imagine that if one round of the possible responses of the light bulbs operating according to the instructions were to happen every second, the entire time needed for this experiment would be a hundred trillion times the age of the universe!

Kauffman was convinced, however, that sooner rather than later, a pattern would be repeated because of an inherent sense of order in the universe. He could not afford to wait too long because he had a limited grant for the computer he was using. He was hoping to get an answer before he lost access to the computer.

The results of his experiment were amazing. Sixteen different possible rounds of the light bulbs completed themselves. The seventeenth round, however, repeated the tenth, the eighteenth repeated another, etc., until four repeating patterns emerged.[14] Rather than out-of-control random behavior, order emerged—a pattern. If order could appear this quickly, then perhaps it is not so extraordinary that life forms developed on earth. The thought of patterns or order inherent in the universe, rather than utter randomness, is a great sign of hope.

I keep bumping into the importance of pattern recognition in the most unexpected places. Lately, I have been involved in the construction of several homes, including my own. In designing our home, my partner and I first had to look at the patterns of our behavior before we could adequately design a home that would serve our needs. For instance, a bath is a sacred event for my partner. It demands time and an aesthetic environment. Therefore, we designed our bathroom to contain no toilet (as in Japanese homes where the toilet has its own separate place), to include space for plants and candles, and to be isolated from other areas of high activity in the house.

Even though our home is not constructed according to the methods of conventional framing—we are using straw bale construction—there are patterns of building that remain the same as those who are building according to the traditional method. In fact, those of us building our own homes have found great help in the work of the architect Christopher Alexander. He has discovered that buildings around the world conform to similar patterns, even though the content of the building materials themselves may change. "And each law or pattern is itself a pattern of relationships among still other laws, which are themselves just patterns of relationships again."[15]

These building patterns emerge because of the similarity worldwide of human behavior. Even though we human beings technically can do an infinite variety of activities every single minute of the day, in reality we operate in life according to certain patterns that are similar around the globe. Human beings have patterns of sleep, cleanliness, celebrations, relationship to fire, etc. "There are surprisingly few of these patterns of events in any one person's way of life, perhaps no more than a dozen."[16]

Pattern recognition is new to Western civilization, but it is not new for indigenous cultures. Historically, they have been more concerned with relationships and patterns than isolated entities. Their study of plants, for instance, involved observation of when plants bloomed, which had fruit and when, what animals ate what parts of the plant and when, how the colors related to the season and the ingestion by other animals, and what stages of development interfaced with what seasons. They even noticed that certain species might disappear for a time or occur in cycles over years. These changes of patterns gave them the information they needed to exist in relationship to the rest of creation.[17] Native American Indians, for example, saw the land and all its creatures as their "relations," and they lived harmoniously with the land for thousands of years prior to our arrival.

> Rising Sun of the Western Sioux tribe considered the so-called scientific view of the white man as inadequate precisely because it did not help people know how to live meaningful lives.[18]

The Newtonian mindset has led us to see ourselves as separate individuals, an outlook that has brought us to the verge of ecological disaster in just over a hundred years precisely because we have lost sight of our relationships. John Muir, one of the few in Western culture who saw the significance of relationships, succinctly put it this way: "When you try to pick anything out by itself, we find it hitched to everything else."

Myron Kellner-Rogers, a consultant to major corporations, recounts a story that conveys the significance of patterns of relationship to the understanding of community.[19] While traveling to one of his assignments, he found himself waiting in an airport terminal idly staring at the news. Suddenly his mind was caught by a news story from a village near Milan, Italy. In this village the average cholesterol count was three hundred, very high by today's standards of health, and yet the average lifespan was eighty years of age, and there was not one recorded instance of heart attack.

The news story went on to relate that when the medical researchers caught wind of this paradox, they descended upon the Italian village to discover the secret of their good health. The researchers decided the answer must lie in isolating the individual gene responsible for dealing with the cholesterol. They worked and worked on isolating the gene and finally did so.

Meanwhile, in the background of all the information about the gene study, the news channel continued flashing pictures of the villagers' daily lives across the screen. The consultant who was watching the news story could see the villagers rising early in the morning, going out fishing, and working in the fields together. There was a tight sense of community and family. They worked hard with each other. At lunch time they gathered together and feasted on bread, pasta, wine, and cheese, and then headed back out to the fields together, working hard again until they all gathered to feast at dinner time, where they would joke, and sing, and carry on.

The research scientists, and the reporting news channel, thought they had solved the mystery by isolating the gene, but the consultant thought differently. He surmised that if any one of those people from the village were to be taken and dropped into Chicago or New York, or even Rome, they would have a heart attack sooner rather than later. According to this consultant, who was operating within the mindset of the new paradigm, the key to the villagers' long and healthy lives lay in their *relationships*, in their community ties—not in their individual genes. The news channel and the scientists had missed the point. The scientific isolation of the gene accomplished little for the health of humanity, precisely because the focus was on artificially isolating parts of life rather than seeking meaningful relationships.

The miracle of this Italian village was that these people had learned to value their relationships, no matter what the day's chaos might bring. Their ability to dance these relationships meaningfully day in and day out as a community was a practice of the Cloudhand.

Against all the odds of the Newtonian paradigm, pattern recognition in relationships, like grass through pavement, is sprouting up in such diverse areas as business, architecture, addiction studies, physics, and biology. Once we begin to focus on relationships—the betweenness of existence—rather than the content or objectifying of existence, an entirely different way of living emerges.

PATTERN

ETHICS

I picked up the young couple at a priest's home just across the border into Mexico at the early dawn. Their two young children, a five- and an eight-year-old, male and female, were with them. The young man was a professor of agriculture in El Salvador and had been arrested and tortured by the National Guard there for having a book in his library about agriculture in Cuba. His wife was a nurse and, unknown to me at the moment, suffering from the mumps. My job as part of the "Sanctuary Movement" was to guide them undetected across the open desert into the United States. They would then be put into a safehouse situation with a local church congregation until it was possible for them to return safely to their native El Salvador.

If I were caught doing this deed, I could go to jail for five years for each member of the family. I would go to jail because transporting illegal aliens was wrong, regardless of my motivation, regardless of my relationship to this situation. For the El Salvadoran family, the consequences would be more severe: If the family were caught, they would be returned to El Salvador where the husband faced certain death.

In the Western mindset or Newtonian worldview, ethical systems have always emphasized decision-making based on the content or details of the dilemma. Traditionally, ethical decisions have been prescribed and proscribed on the basis of the particulars of a predicament. In the case of the El Salvadoran refugees, trying to protect life in an unjust time did not fit the proscribed ethics of what was "right" and what was "wrong."

I was prepared to go to jail on the refugees' behalf, but fortunately, we were not caught. It was not an easy trip, however. We were forced to take a detour when we unexpectedly came across some ranch hands on a hillside. The little boy fell and put his hand into a cactus—without a whimper. We successfully avoided rattle-snakes, scorpions, gila monsters, cowboys, and the border patrol to arrive safely at an elderly Quaker woman's pickup waiting for us on the other side. We were hot, tired, and thirsty—but safe.

Historically, our ethical systems have been based on deline-ating in great detail what can and cannot be done, rather than focusing on a preferred or acceptable way of relating to the world or to one another. The 1960s were a turning point, if not the death of, prior ethical systems in the United States. The content of people's lives were changing so radically and so quickly that ethical systems based on data several hundred, if not several thousand, years old had no relevancy to the sixties generation. Who cared about eating shellfish, wearing the color red, mixing textures of clothing, "mankind" being fruitful and multiplying, slaves being faithful to masters, or women being subordinate to their husbands, as was found in the moral code of Jewish/Christian heritage? It was an entirely different world out there. This generation learned to question the authority of its time but was unable to discover its own sense of authority.

The United States was not alone in having trouble with its ethical basis. Two good friends of mine, brothers from Germany, one of whom is a practicing attorney in Germany and the other now a Canadian citizen working with young children, have both been extensively involved in the nonviolence movement. They contend that World War II was the turning point for the ethical basis of their native country. Along with other Germans of their generation, they believe their parents exposed the pitfalls of an ethical system with spirituality as its basis. For them, ethics must be based on something other than the spiritual, since the warped spiritual fervor of Hitler fanned the flames of Nazism. When I explained to my German friends that one of the leaders in the nonviolent work in America was the Catholic Worker Movement comprised of mostly young people who came to their nonviolent convictions from their interpretation of Christianity, they expressed deep concern. They feared that any movement based on spiritual belief could get out of hand, just as Nazism had gotten out of hand. Yet, neither have found any other equally gripping ethical construct for themselves.

A similar situation has developed among the post-World War II generation of the Japanese. When the emperor was defeated and lost face, spirituality in Japan was dealt a brutal blow. Many people became aspiritual. The Japanese young people that I met in the nonviolent movement in Japan believed that spirituality is reserved for old and old-fashioned people. During my travels in Japan, I saw many Shinto temples in disrepair, except in the more rural areas where aging priests or magicians still maintained them. There was no common ethical construct. For example, the Japanese leadership against the nuclear industry included Communist party members, survivors of Hiroshima and Nagasaki, a large chain of health food cooperatives, and localized environmental groups.

In each of these countries—the United States, Germany, Japan—the ethical systems depended on a content of what was "right" and "wrong," and each ethical system was proven inadequate during a time of turmoil. If we continue to use an ethical construct that focuses on content, on particulars, on specifics, we become lost in the infinite prescription of behavior that will never cover enough territory. There is too much happening. We are adrift in a vast sea of indecisiveness and sparring private interest groups. We are overloaded with details and particulars.

Imagine all the particular concerns: Should we cut down any more trees, and if so, how many? Are there limits to garbage production and destruction? Who decides? Do we let murderers live? Even serial murderers? Whom should we love and when and how often and under what situations? Should we allow casual sex between a man and a woman? Between two men? Between two teenagers? Do we support revolutions, even if the emerging power has nuclear weapons? Do we allow abortion? Euthanasia? Do we allow genetic engineering for test-tube babies? Who will be responsible for such children? Who will answer their questions of "who am I?" The medical world alone is creating new ethical dilemmas at an alarming rate with each advance in medical technology.

To deal with all these questions, we do not need proscriptive or prescriptive content but rather a worldview that centers us in relationship to one another in a manner that is meaningful. We need to focus not on the content of situations but on the nature of our relationships. We need to identify the *patterns* of behavior at work and respond accordingly with what I call "pattern ethics."

Normal science, normal religion, normal education can and do reveal details that clarify patterns for us. But if we allow only normal science, normal religion, normal education to be the basis of our decision-making, we fall into the trap of "representing" interpretations from logical, abstract constructs of someone else for someone else and accepting them unquestionably. If we allow only the approach of normal science, then we assume a normal solution and select one normal solution from a long list of particulars that was used by someone else for something else, regardless of the fit. This is the way law books replace wisdom, doctrine and dogma replace spiritual experience, and technicians replace students in the pursuit of truth.

In one rural community a good friend of mine was the mental health worker for the county. He was very compassionate and conscientious, a former priest. He worked under a particular set of rules: In order to secure payment from the government for his services, he had to categorize, regardless of appropriateness, anyone he counseled according to the *Diagnostic and Statistical Manual of Mental Disorders* (DSM), a government-approved list of mental illness categories. The government would pay for only designated illnesses, not for general, though necessary, counseling for such problems as struggling through a divorce or child-rearing.

If a person came into his office with a problem that did not constitute any form of mental illness, and that person could *pay* for that counseling, no categorization or record-keeping was necessary (other than what my friend wanted for memory's sake) since no government reimbursement was involved. If, however, a person of low-income came into his office with a problem that did not constitute any form of mental illness, and this person could *not* afford to pay for the counseling, a major ethical problem arose. The counseling was equally important for the person of low income as it was for the person who could afford to pay. Yet my friend was forced to assign these clients to one of the DSM categories, even though it would mean his clients would have a mental illness record that could be used against them in future employment or custody hearings. He always chose the most innocuous category he could. Nevertheless, it was a potentially damaging act for the client.

This is a system that tries to force one solution to provide particular answers to every problem—but there were simply too many circumstances that the solution cannot account for. Not only do we *not* need to have a preconceived list of particular solutions to any problem, we no longer need "the work of the 'universal intellectual,' the person who develops an ideal construction of what thought and actions should be."[1]

The problem with universalization of anyone's experience is that whoever is standing at the center of that universe provides the standard against which all other experience is measured. For years, ethical thought has been dominated by white, male, Western civilization—in essence, the ethics of the dominant Jewish/Christian culture. This has caused major problems for individuals and communities not a part of this dominant group because, when a person is privileged to live within the dominant group, it is particularly difficult to see how its standard affects others.

Ethical systems in the old paradigm tend to revolve around unspoken standards or assumptions. For example, for years it was the practice of newspapers to identify the race of a person only if that person were non-white. The accepted standard was that people were assumed to be white unless designated otherwise. This meant that an article would note if a criminal were black, but no notation would be made if a criminal were white. Since articles never pointed out when a criminal was white, it was easy to lapse into the lazy assumption that most criminals were black.

When invisible standards reign, the assumption is made

that all people desire to be within the dominant worldview. But that is certainly not the reality. There are many distinct and flourishing cultures among people of color, women, developing or "two-thirds" world people that carry a legacy of integrity and beauty, and these cultures desire to be nothing other than themselves. For instance, historically, white settlers in North America assumed that all Indians needed the white man's education; therefore, with the best of ethical intentions, though often forcefully, they gave the Indian their "white" education. If an Indian did not want the white man's education, it was assumed that the Indian was ignorant, not well-informed about this option. Consider the perspective of the Seneca chiefs in their response to the "generous bequest left to William and Mary College by a wealthy member of the Virginia gentry to educate Indians."[2]

> We know that you highly esteem the kind of learning taught in those colleges. But, you who are wise must know that the different nations have different conceptions of things; and you will not, therefore, take it amiss if our ideas of this kind of education happen not to be the same with yours.

> Several of our young men were formerly brought up at the colleges of the northern provinces; they were instructed in all your sciences; but when they came back to us they were bad runners, ignorant of every means of living in the woods, unable to bear either cold or hunger, knew neither how to build a cabin, take a deer or kill an enemy; spoke our language imperfectly—they were, therefore, neither fit for hunters, warriors nor counselors. They were totally good for nothing.

> We are, therefore, not the less obliged by your kind offer, though we decline the accepting of it; and, to show our grateful sense of it, if the gentlemen of Virginia will send us a dozen of their sons, we will take care to their education, instruct them in all that we know, and make men of them.[3]

We often universalize without realizing it. I think of the time when I toured with the human sexuality task force of the United Methodist Church in the Colorado Conference. We made a conscious effort to have at least one gay or lesbian person on our team. The workshop participants assumed we were all heterosexual and were shocked to find out, in the course of our sharing together, that there was a gay or lesbian on the team. The shock was not that the gay or lesbian was so different, but that he or she was so obviously just like everyone else. If a gay person had problems, the assumption had been that the problems arose *because* the person was gay, not because the person had problems like anyone else.

The universalization of one class of people, such as heterosexuals, as "good" and another class of people, such as homosexuals, as "bad" is yet another attempt to provide one "solution" that would apply to every set of circumstances. The point is that ethical problems exist as a result of patterns of behavior, regardless of the details of race, gender, religion, or sexual orientation.

The desire for prescribed ethics, that is, as content set down in detail, arises from our *fear of chaos*, from our fear of loss of control. As a culture, we have projected evil onto chaos precisely because of our inability to control it. If we would focus on "dancing" the relationships (the essence of *t'ai chi*) rather than controlling the content of our lives, the concepts of chaos and ethics would take on entirely different dimensions, regardless of the particularities.

If we would begin our decision-making by establishing a simple pattern of relationship, then like the simple pattern of a fractal that unfolds *ad infinitum*, this would provide *the basis of an infinitely complex way of unfolding in the world.*

When I attended the Berkana Institute, a think-tank relating the new sciences to business management,[4] I was in a room with approximately thirty other high-powered business consultants. We dialogued with each other for three days by following three simple rules: 1) speak only for yourself, truthfully; 2) include what has already been said; and 3) seek to expand the inquiry. During that entire time, no one dominated, and no one felt left out. At times, thoughts were shared so fast that it was like popcorn bouncing around the room. At other times, our thoughts would sift into a pregnant silence. It was an amazing process to watch unfold. We could never have successfully controlled such a discussion if we had tried. And we could never have achieved the insights that we carried home with us if we had planned the agenda.

In a similar fashion, if we would focus not on the control of particular behavior but on the pattern of our lives, we would have infinite possibilities of response to ethical dilemmas, each unique to our situation. Each response, though spontaneous, even chaotic, would nevertheless would be contained or embraced within a pattern of relationship. It is not that the details do not have a place in decision-making, but it is that the details *do* have their place—and a rather limited place it is. If we would focus not on what we are doing but how we are relating, not on judging the content of our behavior but on the nature of our relationships, we would shift from an ethical system driven by the need to be in control to a new ethics based on the experience of being in relationship in the unique unfolding of the now. We would discover that, like the fractal where there are infinite patterns within patterns, there are infinite, unique paths for each and every person that do not intersect, do not repeat, and do not negate each other.

For much of my adult life, I have felt called into ministry, even the priesthood, based on my belief in the sanctity of life and my desire to foster that sanctity in the world. Initially, I had assumed this meant that at some point I must become an ordained minister or priest. Meanwhile, every avenue toward ordination was thwarted. People suggested that I be a lawyer, a librarian, or a teacher, but nothing resonated with my inner journey.

Frustrated, I had begun to believe that my inability to settle into some role was a sign of major dysfunction on my part. In the course of a local pending election, however, I was asked to run for political office. That prospect had never crossed my mind. (Our culture does not exactly consider the role of the politician a spiritual matter.) When I considered running for the office, though, my heart responded in such a way that I knew I had to try. For me at this time, formal politics has turned out to be a perfect fit. Although I do not overtly engage in any form of ministry or religious behavior, I do bring a relationship to my work that reflects my spiritual base. It is not what I do that determines ministry, but how I relate, and the ability to trust in the infinite unfolding of the journey.

If each of us is true to our own unique unfolding, our own unique creation, our paths will not cross or negate one another's. It is precisely when we try to control our paths, to copy or model our path on someone else's, to reject our own uniqueness, that our paths suddenly become destructive.

If evil were to be seen not as the content of an act but as the nature of a relationship, evil would resemble chaos less and entropy more. Entropy is absolute randomness in which there is no differentiation, no identity, no naming, no uniqueness, no possibility, no contained pattern or image. Author and storyteller Madeleine L'Engle provides just such a metaphor for evil in her depiction of the *ecthroi* in her fantasy *A Wind in the Door*. The *ecthroi* creatures delight in namelessness, in indistinguishability, and destruction. When the characters in the story decide to enter into relationship with one another, rather than focus on what in particular should be done to combat the *ecthroi*, evil loses its grip.[5]

Even the littlest decisions from our experience of being in relationship can have profound reverberations throughout the universe, the consequences of which we can only imagine. I am continually amazed, for example, when reminded that the mass of the universe is composed almost entirely—99%—of just two elements, hydrogen and helium. Many scientists believe that in the beginning of the cosmos there was great uniformity. What we observe today as our universe may be the result of a quantum fluctuation, the tiniest blip or flutter (or heartbeat?) of energy exchange in a vacuum. Such an event may have precipitated the "big bang," resulting in a universe composed primarily of the two elements, hydrogen and helium.[6] From something incredibly simple and relatively uniform came the complexity and infinite variety of our present universe. Even the simplest of interactions is capable of unfolding into infinite possibility.

Edward Lorenz, fascinated with his weather research, experimented with simulating weather conditions on his computer in an attempt to predict weather. One day while running some statistics, he entered an equation into his computer program only to three decimal points, rather than to the entire six, as a shortcut. The original number was .506127, and he entered only .506, assuming that weather cannot significantly be affected by one part in ten thousand. How could the earth be affected by such a tiny difference? How finely tuned was the earth after all? The result was a weather pattern that quickly became totally different. One very simple, tiny difference changed the entire pattern.[7] It was as if the air disturbed by the wings of a butterfly could change the weather around the world. This is popularly known as the "butterfly effect." The butterfly effect is as true for our behavior as it is for anything else. The littlest act of our day may, unknown to us, reverberate throughout the universe.

When I first began to preach, I assumed that preaching was a one-way affair where I imparted important knowledge and insight, and the congregation simply soaked it up. I was young and arrogant. During one sermon, I noticed a member of the congregation wince at something I said. In registering that simple wince, I realized that preaching was a dance between the congregation and the preacher. I was never able to preach again without being aware that I was part of a community that had as much to teach me as I had to teach. That one simple wince changed my preaching—and my life.

Even our most meager actions or inactions are enfolded and unfolded in the universe. We can see this in the Mandelbrot set where the whole image or pattern is found repeated over and over within the infinite parts. This is also true in a hologram where laser light technology projects an image in three dimensions into any space. If any one part of the hologram is studied, it is possible to see the entire image in that part. Physicist David Bohm also believes that the hologram is model for understanding the structure of the universe.[8] L'Engle's fantasy A *Wind in the Door* makes this point as well. In this story, it is the ethical decisions of the tiniest farandolae—parts of a single cell—that protect the health of a whole boy, and, ultimately, the entire universe.[9]

Although each unique person walks different particulars, which have profound consequences in unexpected ways, there are nevertheless familiar patterns, familiar relationships that we have in common. We are already capable of sharing familiar ethical understandings, such as "murder is not acceptable," "children should be loved," "beauty and honesty are valued." As we each reach deeper into our pursuit of truth, our spiritual journeys, we discover familiar patterns among races, among faiths (whether Buddhist,

American Indian, Wiccan, Hindu, Christian), among nationalities, across boundaries within our own communities.

The Vietnamese Buddhist monk Thich Nhat Hanh, Mahatma Gandhi, Jesus of Nazareth, Dorothy Day, Martin Luther King, Jr., for example, are renowned for their commitment to a pattern of behavior, a way of entering into relationships commonly referred to in the English language as "nonviolence." Another perhaps more accurate translation for the Hindu word *satyagraha* is "truth-force,"[10] rather than nonviolence. Nonviolence as a pattern of relating is not tied to results, nor to time. It is not the end that is important, but the means. In the words of pacifist A.J. Muste, "There is no way to peace. Peace is the way."[11] Or in the words of Jacques Maritain, "the means are 'in a sense the end in process of becoming.' "[12] The focus is not on outcome but on a pattern of being. There is an emphasis on the necessity of practice, over and over again, to enable this way of relating to become truly alive, vital, real.

When I have trained people in nonviolence, whether in a schoolyard in the Occupied Territories or in the bunkhouse of a Kansas cattle ranch, prescriptive behavior plays a very minor role, while creativity and uniqueness of response is critical. The focus of the training is to encourage the participants to enter into a way of relating, not a list of DOs and DON'Ts. The content, the details, are very different, but there remains a common pattern.

The shared pattern of nonviolence depends on a heart-felt journey of faith by each participant (whether Buddhist, indigenous, Christian, or other) regarding the sanctity of life, the sacredness of the universe. Central to a nonviolent way of relating is the belief that no one of us has an exclusive corner to the truth, and that each of us has a part of it; that in any situation there is an infinitely creative force present advocating on every behalf to "work it out"—despite what might seem an irresolvable dilemma or confrontation; and that the "truth-force" is not external to us, nor confined within us, but rather we are intimately enfolded with it.

Moreover, what is most important to sustaining nonviolence is not to concentrate on the external conflicts "out there" alone, but to draw parallels or patterns from those external conflicts to those similar conflicts that reside within ourselves. We need to make every effort to surface personal fears that may result in unconscious behavior that we then rationalize for something else. For instance, I used to dislike babysitting infants. I used to rationalize those feelings by saying that infants were too dependent for my personality. Later I realized that I disliked caring for infants because my own mother had found my infancy to be a very trying time. I had carried that unconscious awareness into my adulthood. My dislike of caring for infants disappeared when I was able to surface my unconscious feelings.

In the words of the thirteenth-century mystic Meister Eckhart, "whatever can be truly expressed in its proper meaning must emerge from inside a person and pass through the inner form. It cannot come from outside to inside of a person but must emerge from within."[13] The external situation is reflected within each of us and is intimately interrelated, regardless of the particulars, according to a pattern of relationship. If we seek alignment with the pattern, with the relationship—not the content—infinite creative options arise for every circumstance. This is the essence of "pattern ethics."

Perhaps one way to understand this more is to see pattern ethics in action. In 1992 I facilitated an international nonviolent peace march in Israel and the Occupied Territories, and acted as one of its nonviolent trainers. The participants were drawn from those already known to be committed to nonviolence in their own lives. They were very ordinary people from all walks of life. Prior to coming to Israel, the participants had committed themselves to undergoing extensive education about the conflict between Israel and the Occupied Territories from the perspective of both sides.

During the course of the nonviolent training, we stressed the principles—the patterns of relating—of nonviolence. We divided ourselves into small support groups or "affinity" groups. We were all aware that it was a most volatile situation, and though we were serious in our intentions to escalate worldwide concern for the struggle between the Israelis and Palestinians, we did not want to escalate the violence. We encouraged participants to explore their personal fears around the proposed action. We practiced nonviolence in role plays that confronted our biggest fears. Relationships developed within the affinity groups, between the spokespeople from each of these affinity groups, and with local Israeli Jews and

Palestinians. These relationships were ultimately the key to this nonviolent action.

One hot afternoon in June, a group of approximately one hundred eighty people from Europe, India, Africa, North America, Japan, Israel, and Palestine began to move toward the infamous "green line" between Israel and the Occupied Territories. Three lines of defense, one of which was the Israeli National Defense Force, an ominous group for any of us, faced us. We had stressed in the training that the people in uniform were not the enemy but, rather, people with whom we needed to develop some form of relationship. We needed to take the concern we had for each other into the greater world, most especially in the face of the most threatening violence.

This was far from easy. There were language barriers, cultural barriers, religious barriers, and ideological barriers. Each affinity group was free to act as they needed. It would have been impossible for our international group to agree to any single content or prescribed behavior. We could only hope to agree to a pattern of relating.

The dance of chaos unfolded, according to the pattern of nonviolence. All marchers who could not risk arrest or violent encounter with the authorities (pregnant women, for example) were asked to leave the site. They were to be available to provide support later for anyone who might be arrested or hurt. Palestinians without Israeli citizenship were asked to return to their homes, in order to both pre-empt potential reactionary behavior on the part of some Palestinians and to prevent later retaliatory behavior toward Palestinians by certain Israelis.

Some cavalry were present, and there was some concern that people might be trampled. Unknown to the whole, one affinity group felt drawn to the cavalry and took it upon themselves to disarm this small group of mounted soldiers. A member of this affinity group, a young man from Scotland, pulled out his bagpipes, began playing, and walked right up to the faces of the horses while the rest of the group gathered around him and sat down. Horses cannot trample what is facing them and will not trample people sitting or lying down. This action had a calming effect on the demonstrators.

Just prior to the formal crossing of the "green line," another affinity group had walked slightly across the line but out into an open field obviously to seek shade under a tree while they waited. When the march did begin, they simply kept walking through the field, finally encountering the main road around a bend where they were met by the highest level of security—and the most feared. A Buddhist monk and a Roman Catholic priest were members of this group. The monk bowed before the security force and offered a blessing via chant and drumming. The guards responded well but complained to the priest about the monk's incessant drumming. When the priest agreed that the drumming was equally hard on his nerves, the priest and the guards quickly found common ground.

Several other groups started to cross the "green line" in an orderly manner. The initial response from the arresting officials was very rough. The first nonviolent demonstrators arrested absorbed bruised ribs and gravel burns. However, the officials could not sustain such violence in the face of the obviously calm, yet determined, affinity groups that refused to react.

The patterns continued to unfold as the marchers were transported to various containment points. An Israeli soldier guarding the marchers on one bus confessed that the same blood ran in the veins of the Palestinians as the Israelis, and it was a sad commentary that they were in such conflict. Another Israeli soldier carried a young Israeli Jewish boy cradled in his arms all the way to the retaining bus. A prison guard noticed that I was admiring his cup of Turkish coffee and surreptitiously brought me one where I was sitting alone. When a young man from Princeton stood up for his constitutional rights, according to the Israeli's own system, by not handing over his passport, he was hit hard in the head and smashed against the prison wall by an angry guard. The young man's fellow prisoners did not accost the violent guard, but started chanting, "The whole world is watching!" The women, hearing the chant through the walls, responded by requesting that the young man be checked by one of our own doctors. The Israeli guard in charge promptly agreed to this and removed the angry guard from duty.

In the course of the entire forty-eight hours of arrest and prison time, Israel received calls from El Salvador to Belgium inquiring on our behalf. All of a sudden there were new relationships forming around the world with Israel, whether among the citizens of various countries that had been strangers to one another, or between Israelis and Palestinians. An Israeli reserve soldier, who had himself been stoned by young Palestinian males, dared to march and go to his own prison along with these international visitors, including a neighboring Palestinian. He was joined by other equally committed Israeli Jews. Fear on all sides was overcome. Violence that was ready and waiting was defused. That which had been hidden for many was brought out into the light. A gesture of peace had prevailed.

Well-intentioned people had obeyed the orders of their beloved country Israel. Well-intentioned people had broken the law. The point of the encounter was not that one person was right and another wrong. The point of the encounter was neither the content, nor a particular solution, but the uncovering of what had been festering outside of many people's awareness and the developing of creative relationships among everyday people to solve the dilemma. Community emerged that hot June day along the "green line."

Under the old paradigm, this situation would have resulted in serious violence. In fact, those functioning within the old paradigm had expected violence. Ambulances had been brought by the authorities for the event. The marchers had been surrounded by clenched fists. As with Gandhi, or Martin Luther King, Jr., however, there was a belief held by the marchers that they did not have to settle for violence, either toward themselves or between Palestinians and Israelis. They believed that with careful preparation and practice, in the face of the worst fears, a creative force would arise among them in response to the occasion and work it out somehow. The marchers merely needed to dare to dance out the relationships as beautifully and chaotically as the Cloudhand, their very lives on the line.

"Pattern ethics" is based on a profound faith that affirms infinite possibility exists—*and* can be trusted. That there is a pattern in which infinite possibility is embraced. That there is a purpose. That it is *relationship* that is of consequence. That the particularities are only important as they relate to the whole, to the relationships. And that when these relationships are respected, a new and greater whole emerges.

EMERGENCE

*A*t the beginning of life forms, there were bacteria. Most of us think about bacteria as the mysterious things my mother ominously called "germs." But bacteria are amazing in that they are so simple and yet so powerful. Bacteria are merely a collection of parts in unfettered relationships. They easily transfer their parts with other bacteria in unnerving and everchanging combinations. There are few set boundaries. At the level of bacteria, indistinguishability reigns. In studying the work of biologist Lynn Margulis, author William Irwin Thompson discovered that bacteria were

> . . . collective entities whose membranes were not walls but vehicles of transport and communication. Bacteria were social creatures who could exchange genes promiscuously and with such a rapid rate of mutation that they were better understood as a 'superorganism' of planetary dimensions, in other words a planetary bioplasm.[1]

These tiny bacteria that most of us never see, and yet go to great lengths to avoid, are responsible for changing the course of history.

At some point in time, bacteria made a major change in how they operated with one another. Instead of "everyone" doing everything, these bacteria entered into restricted or contractual relationships with one other. Certain bacteria opted to deal with food production, others restrained themselves to live within a more confined solid membrane to become a nucleus, and others carried waste. Then, and only then, from the cooperative efforts of the bacteria, a truly new "individual" emerged—the cell. Unlike the bacteria, the cell that emerged was capable of sexuality, birth, and death.[2]

This monumental jump from nondescript bacteria to the first cell epitomizes the controversial subject of evolution. There is no field of study that has *not* been affected by the assumptions derived from this jump from bacteria to the cell. There are no jobs or organizations that remain unaffected by these assumptions. Yet most of us are not consciously aware of what these assumptions are.

The Buddha teaches that it is necessary to stop and meditate on life in order to see the assumptions that lie at its base. He admonishes us in particular to notice the impermanency and interdependence of all being, whether as rock, tree, or human being. Physicist Brian Swimme says it even more poetically:

> When you walk into a forest, learn to tremble with the magnitude of what you are about. . . . Sip a cup of coffee the next morning, and all the fir trees grow warm. . . . If you develop even the least flicker of sensitivity, the universe will come alive within you.[3]

The Buddha stresses that if we will but take the time to meditate on the paradoxes, we will discover the secret of the universe, and our suffering will cease.

We cannot underestimate the suffering that has resulted from the misunderstanding of this journey from the simple to the more complex. If we take a little time and patience to really ponder the leap from bacteria to cell, we, too, could discover a secret of the universe, and much suffering could be alleviated.

When the simple bacteria became a more complex organism by exercising limits according to certain patterns of relationships, these limitations gave form or uniqueness. Picture a nondescript lump of clay. It can become either a bowl, plate, or mug when form and limits are imposed. The clay as a mug is no longer interchangeable with the clay as a plate. Nor is the mug more or less valuable than the plate. They are simply different for different needs.

Likewise, the human being is the result of limitations and patterns of relationship for the purpose of establishing a figure—say the figure of myself, Rhea—in the universe. Certain cells are restricted to carrying blood, others to handling the nervous system, and yet others to forming bones, all of which eventually give form to the human being. The way these limitations combine or organize distinguish who we are. We are no more or less valuable than another, nor are we interchangeable. We offer different gifts for different needs, based on our own uniqueness. All complex forms depend on establishing boundaries of behavior among the simpler forms. *Complexity is not a matter of higher development, but the organization of limitations.*

I think of this organization a little like various sports. Although volleyball and basketball use a different ball and net, the real differences between the games are the patterns of relating between team members and the ball. The players decide to organize, each taking on a function best suited to their skills, and act according to the rules of the sport. By restricting their relationships according to a set of instructions, or patterns of behavior, they become a volleyball team or a basketball team. The more limited the way of acting, the greater is the distinctiveness or particularity of performance—in this case, a specific sports team.

In the same way, as certain bacteria gather together and organize according to a particular need to function, a distinctiveness of organism is produced—in this case, a cell. Certain cells gather to make certain tissues, such as muscles, which make certain organs, such as the heart, which make certain systems, such as the circulatory system, which make the human body.

The paradox is that we cannot "evolve" to become more complex without giving up certain powers. This turns the concept of hierarchy on its head. That which we are moving toward is no more significant than that which we have been. Each new development is the natural outcome of need for further function. For instance, a human being cannot run as fast, nor is she as strong, as four-footed animals, but we can make tools to create our dreams, which is far different from four-footed animals. Our tools also meet the need of making us less dependent on speed and brawn. Each new development is the result of a change in context, from which new needs arise, in the process of further unfolding.

We used to think that the cells of muscles and the cells of blood and the cells of bones differed because of the different genes in them. "Yet it is now also clear that all the cells in an organism contain roughly the *same* genetic instructions. *Cell types differ because they have dissimilar patterns* of genetic activity, not because they have different genes."[4] Just as basketball differs from volleyball not so much by the difference in balls, but in the way the game is played, so, too, is Nature defined not so much by a change of content (type of ball), or expansion of parts (number of players on the team), but by the patterns of relating (the way the game is played).

Clearly, our more complex forms are indebted to the simpler forms. Our bodies still carry the simpler forms, including the oldest bacteria. The content of our bodies, the particulars—bone, blood, and breath—are not so different from that of our predecessors, but our way of relating to the world is vastly different. In a very tangible way we are intimately connected to all life forms that have preceded us. Rather than a feeling of superiority, this awareness engenders a feeling of sincere gratitude.

Likewise, a sports team is indebted to its players. While performing as a team, individuals exhibit qualities of sacrifice, discipline, understanding, competency, and vision that they may not exhibit in the classroom or at home. They choose to limit what they eat, when they practice, and when they rest. They voluntarily give up the right to come and go as they please because they resonate with a common desire, that is, being a winning team. They become much more than their individual characteristics. They become a remarkable team of talent, one that senses each other's every move, bonded by a need to function for a specific purpose, that is, winning the game. Together as a team they are more than who they are as individual players or even as individual students. The team comes alive with a palpable sense of identity. *The whole is greater than the sum of its parts.*

The team is not *more* important than the individual players. The team is *different* from the individual players and performs a more specific function. The team is indebted to the decision and commitment of the individual players for its existence. The players are rewarded with a sense of identity, accomplishment, and community that goes far beyond what they could have experienced as individuals. The players come alive in ways they could never have experienced alone.

Too often we have a skewed understanding of who and what is valuable because of the popular understanding of evolution that life progresses from a lesser form to a more valued form on the ladder of hierarchy. This theory of hierarchy is one of the most powerful, if not *the* most powerful, tenet of the Newtonian worldview. These notions of progress and hierarchy are the underpinnings of the Newtonian mindset that values rugged individualism, control, and domination, whether of nature, women, or other races.

According to Harvard zoologist Stephen Jay Gould, we have created this concept of progress to provide meaning for human history,[5] but it is actually "a noxious, culturally embedded, untestable, nonoperational idea that must be replaced if we wish to understand the patterns of history."[6] In other words, we have coined the concept of progress to bolster the human ego against what we perceive as an ever-threatening chaotic world. Gould goes on to point out two of the most disastrous consequences of such an outlook: the theory of racism and the theory of hierarchy of life forms.

When the theory of progress is coupled with the concept of the survival of the fittest, we have the battle of the races. We are all too familiar with the theory that the white race is the high point of creation.[7] In Washington, D.C., the new Holocaust Museum chronicles in horrifying detail the extent to which people have gone to prove white supremacy. Nazism, the massacre of indigenous tribes, and American slavery are but a few examples of where clenched fists have used the theory of progress to rationalize white supremacy.

Another consequence of the theory of progress is the idea that humans are the apex of the hierarchy: "[E]volution, in being viewed as progressing from lower to ever higher forms, was considered to lead unswervingly to the emergence of humans."[8] This has led us to an anthropocentric mindset which, according to novelist Daniel Quinn in *Ishmael*, is a cultural myth that must be exposed for its inadequacy. The myth that the world was made for humans leads to the premise that "it *belongs* to us and we can do what we damn well please with it."[9]

An extreme example of this mindset was played out on the island where I live. A fellow islander was distraught over the fact that a family of otters was crawling up onto his dock and into his boat, leaving a disgusting trail of excrement and shellfish remains. His response to this dilemma was to wire his dock with electrical charge, enhanced by the presence of sea water. When a family of five otters attempted once again to crawl up on the dock, each youngster was electrocuted in turn, followed finally by the mother, all sinking out of sight into the bay waters. The islander felt perfectly justified in this act. After all, otters were only otters, and he was a human being who needed to care first and foremost for his belongings.

The view of the new sciences, on the other hand, is that we are merely one part of an unfolding that will move beyond human beings—indebted to us, yes, but encompassing us as part of a larger, ongoing creation. As significant as human beings are to the earth's journey, we, too, could become one of the victims of mass extinctions. In fact, to gain a bit of perspective, "99.9 per cent of all species that have ever lived are now extinct."[10] The new worldview humbles our understanding of ourselves. Yet we are reluctant to let go of the theory of progress, of the idea that we are the pinnacle of creation.

But the reality is that the Newtonian concept of hierarchy is inadequate for the needs and crises of our time. We need to see differently now, with an entirely new dimension of seeing—not because we are becoming more valuable beings, but because our unfolding, our need, demands that we do so. We need to engage in new relationships.

Just as bacteria can form relationships and create the cell, they can also form a different set of relationships and create an organism known as a parasite. One particular parasite lives in the body of a termite. No single bacteria or microbe alone can consume wood and produce the acetate that the termite wants. However, when certain of the bacteria enter into relationship with one another, they can consume wood and produce as a by-product what is most pleasing to the termite.[11] Five microbes of three different varieties, when assigned to specific tasks, make one parasite. These five microbes can accomplish infinitely more in relationship as a parasite than an entire colony of microbes can as individuals. *The point at which the whole becomes greater than the sum of its parts is "emergence."* Emergence is the result of a gathering of individuals that enter into restricted or limited relationship with one another in such a way that a further function is accomplished.

This new function, that defines the parasite beyond simply being a conglomeration of five microbes, is called its *emergent quality*. Emergent qualities are different, new, and awesome, not due to new parts, but due to new restricted relationships. The microbes made minor adjustments, that is, minor interior changes in their new role as a parasite. But for every small change in detail, there were exponentially more interrelationships created. Despite only minor changes in detail, these microbes related, not in a *few* new ways, but in *infinitely* more complex and more competent ways as a parasite. It is these relationships that provide the emergent qualities. "The emergent qualities are the interrelationships, which increase exponentially while the number of components increase linearly."[12]

From the perspective of the new paradigm, the human being is not so different in component parts from, say, a bear. Yet the way we relate to the world is infinitely different. The whole is indeed greater than the sum of its parts not due to a hierarchical concept of evolution, but due to this concept of "emergence," or "emergent properties." As Susan Oyama, author of *The Ontogeny of Information*, has observed, "Surely the point is that presence of components is not the same as the system of their *interactions*. It is the latter that constitutes life."[13]

This is a dramatic change of perspective from what most of us have grown up with. We have been taught to equate evolution with the concept of hierarchy, but hierarchy is only one interpretation of evolution. The more time we take examining the concept of emergence, the more fascinating the journey.

Emergence seems to be like a one-way window. We can look from the more complex back toward the simpler and experience understanding; however, it seems to be impossible to look from the position of the simpler toward the complex. For instance, we all know water is created from the elements of hydrogen and oxygen. We can look from water back to hydrogen and oxygen and understand the process of making water. However, if we had never learned about water, had never experienced it, we would have no way to predict that the combination of hydrogen and oxygen would become something liquid. This is one of the characteristics of emergence: *We cannot predict behavior of more complex forms from the qualities of the simpler forms.*[14]

I was taking a college course in the history of the Middle Ages, often pejoratively referred to as the Dark Ages. My professor was a lover of the Middle Ages and conveyed great excitement to the class. Though we students found the professor brilliant and the course challenging, I cannot say any of us could see what she was so excited about.

I had studied faithfully for the final exam and dreaded the process. In the middle of answering one of the final exam questions, I experienced an "Aha!" It dawned on me that the Middle Ages was a time of intense, deep, grass-roots reorganizing of the social fabric. It was a time of immense empowerment of a wider cross-section of people who heretofore had seen themselves only as chattel. They began to resonate with a new quality or dimension of existence. Without this active transition time of the Middle Ages, the Age of Enlightenment would never have arisen.

During the Middle Ages, the Franciscan order was responsible for major education reform and facilitated a grass-roots empowerment that became a significant factor in the emergence of the Renaissance. Though we can look back on the emergence of the Franciscan order, and understand it, we could never have predicted this outcome from simply observing the rag-tag, empty-handed, seemingly eccentric St. Francis of Assisi and friends. In the same way, no one looking at the Middle Ages from within was able to notice the empowerment on so many frontiers at once; nevertheless, society took this leap into the Renaissance that we can see only in hindsight.

Another characteristic of emergence is that *the simpler the form, the more enduring it is*. Researcher and prairie farmer Wes Jackson, in his careful study of emergence, concluded that, "Atoms are more lasting than molecules. The physical and biological components of an ecosystem are more lasting than the ecosystem."[15] In other words, bacteria from the beginning of time may still exist today; however, more complex beings such as the dinosaurs have come and gone.[16]

Jackson also points out the characteristic that the more complex the form, "the smaller the population of instances."[17] For example, it takes millions of cells to produce a few tissues, which make even fewer organs, which culminate in only one body. Complex forms are dependent upon and indebted to many more of the simpler forms. In this respect, the complex forms are more vulnerable to extinction than the more plentiful simpler forms.

Yet another characteristic of emergence is that, like a "critical mass," there seems to be a point at which *the emergent quality arises without warning*.[18] Physics teaches that it is impossible for scientists to observe what is happening with an electron at its lowest quantum state.[19] Initially, there is no way to know from observation when an electron will take its quantum "leap" from one energy mode to another. We can blast an electron with more and more energy without any cumulative effect. Rather, the electron awaits a frequency of energy with which it resonates. This frequency is a matter of quality, not quantity. Not until a certain quality of energy is used with the electron will it move into a higher mode.

A similar situation exists regarding the breaking of glass at certain frequencies of sound. This is not a matter of volume of sound. We can play louder and louder without breaking the glass. But when we use a certain frequency of sound, a certain quality of sound, then, without warning, the glass will break.[20] There is no advance warning of this "leap." We cannot see anything until the leap happens.[21]

We cannot observe what causes simpler organisms to emerge into the more complex. We cannot pinpoint what is contributing to the emergent quality that causes a community, such as a community of bacteria, to leap into greater complexity, such as a parasite. We cannot specify the leap from one state to another from external observation. We cannot make the leap happen by force or coercion.

As that student of the Middle Ages, a lot of "force" had gone into making me understand European history. I had been the repository of an enormous amount of energy from the professor. I was inundated with details. But none of this had made any lasting impression. No amount of energy on the part of the professor, no amount of "force," no matter how kindly or well-intentioned, could substitute for that "Aha!" experience, unexpected, wherein I finally entered into relationship with the people of the Middle Ages and resonated with their times. (I am sure my professor had despaired of my ever gaining that insight.) Not until those details entered into a pattern, a certain quality of relationship, was I able to "see."

As an involved student, I could not predict that this "Aha" would happen, although in hindsight I could see its development. Often we mistake our hindsight for the conscious awareness of knowing or understanding our own development at the time. For instance, years later, historians can tell us the meaning of our efforts, but most of us, absorbed in the moment, are not conscious of all that is happening around us. Full awareness comes only with hindsight.

Part of the reason we cannot predict the threshold of emergence from within the process is because emergence does not follow a linear or logical pathway. One of the characteristics of emergence is that *emergence is not a rational process; it is a chaotic process.* Reductionists, who reduce the world to its individual building blocks and nothing more, tend to see life as a rational process. They believe that if a logical move is presented to us, we will surely do it.

I encountered this belief first-hand in some very vivid moments in Japan. My hosts were absolutely convinced that if they presented me with the logically right way to do things, I would then do it. I, however, being very American and resonating with the American spirit, could have cared less at times about any "right" way. I would simply do it *my* way.

Once, at midnight, we approached a red light. The street

was all of ten feet wide, with no cars within earshot or within my realm of vision. When I chose to cross the street against the light, I appalled my Japanese companion. I was surprised by the intensity of the lecture this act precipitated.

Another incident involved a visit to the public bath. When showering before entering the common bath, I neglected to rub my soap into a lather the consistency of shaving cream to spread all over my naked body. I had used soap over my entire body, but I had not foamed it up into a lather in the Japanese way. Consequently, I had my body scrubbed for me by the reigning matron bathing at the time!

Human beings have never acted entirely from logic. In our decision-making, we unconsciously include our subconscious thoughts and our feelings. How we were raised, whether we have had traumatic encounters, whether we have just smelled a perfume that reminded us of someone or heard a song that put us in a different mood, whether someone reminds us of our ex-spouse—all these contribute to how we behave. This ensures that behavior is hardly a "rational" process and is much more chaotic than we might like to believe. Depth psychology tells us that the unconscious erupts quite often into our behavior, which in the interest of preserving the Newtonian paradigm of reductionism, we then attempt to rationalize.

Our society currently operates under the rule that we must behave logically to be respected. The result of this unspoken rule has been that we rationalize all our actions according to what is socially acceptable at the time. Then we institutionalize our rationalizations. We expend a great deal of energy making very logical constructs to defend what we are feeling. These efforts can become quite convoluted, and they short-circuit our true experience.

For instance, as a small child I wanted to go to the corner drug store to see the "yo-yo" man who had been advertised on our local TV station. I needed a nickel to go. I was never a child to ask for money, and candy or snacks at the corner drug store was not part of my experience growing up. We were quite poor, but not as poor as several of my Dad's parishioners who had dirt floors. Nevertheless, I thought that this out-of-the-ordinary event might merit my receiving a nickel. I was six years old at the time.

My request was denied. I never did see the "yo-yo" man, and I remember being quite saddened by the experience, but I never even thought to appeal the decision. However, as you can tell, the experience stuck with me, and something felt unfair about it, though it was logically consistent with other of my mother's decisions. Later in my adult life, I realized that my mother suffered terribly from the poverty and the insecurity of that poverty. Her decision to deny me the nickel was more a reaction to her own fears and pain than to my meager request.

Many times since I have seen a child be quick to pick up when the parent is responding out of a true concern for the child, and when the parent is responding with a rationalization for his or her own feelings or needs. These encounters erode the authority of the parent with the child because there is no possibility for the child to resonate or have an "Aha!" experience; rationalization denies that possibility.

It is not just individuals who rationalize; society, too, rationalizes its behaviors. For years, and even to this day in some cultures, society has rationalized the lack of education for women. Young women have been denied education not because they are of inferior intelligence or incapable of learning complex material, as these young women have been told, but because the education of women would threaten a change in the social/economic structure. I remember in high school that a female friend was told she must not study to become a veterinarian because it was a man's job. Great lengths have been taken to rationalize this and similar positions, such as the denial of priesthood to women in the Roman Catholic Church. As a culture, we deny ourselves the very opportunities for new relationships that could move us forward to meet the needs of our time.

Our rationalizations and our denial of potential relationships sabotage our future. At these points of deception, we sabotage emergence—whether of ourselves or one another. When we are unable to see or admit that we do behave in ways that go beyond rational or logical constructs, we are unable to acknowledge our needs. Without the ability to acknowledge our needs, we are unable to respond creatively to those needs.

This sabotage is often the direct result of fear. Fear is in and of itself not bad. I have been grateful myself for "friend" fear who has warned me of impending danger, whether on the snowfields of the Rockies, or when encountering a smile at a meeting that did not ring true. Fear is only a warning, and it sends us back to our relationships, our community, our context of belonging, to check out the nature and significance of this fear. In the same way a child, when fear strikes, heads for a trusted sibling, parent, or peer for assurance, or confirmation of that fear. It is when fear moves from being a "friend" to being a "tyrant" in control of our lives that we lose our reference point, our sense of connectedness, our centeredness. When fear is a tyrant, we lose our ability to dance the Cloudhand.

When a group of individuals can face their fears and rationalizations and become intimately interrelated and mutually responsible, an awareness of community emerges. This is happening everywhere. Women, for example, have been gathering together for years at quilting bees, in church basements at potlucks, in the factories during wartime, at PTA meetings, creatively solving problems of local economic development, fund-raising, sending clothing and food to the indigent, patching together cast-off cloth, pulling together the frayed edges of a society all too concentrated on details and content to see the obvious solutions. Their work, unrewarded, unpublicized, unseen, has salvaged more than one community.

Today there is a group in North Carolina called the Piedmont Peace Project. This group believes that nothing significant occurs to create community until people become interrelated to one another in a way that powerfully resonates in each of their own lives. From the outset of any effort, the Piedmont Peace Project pinpoints a geographical area and consults every person in need in that area, regardless of race or belief or gender or financial status. Every person is encouraged to help.

In one very low income inner-city neighborhood, the Project had a goal to obtain a dumpster. The organization's leaders could have contacted affluent friends or influential people, such as a town council member, to put pressure on the city to provide a dumpster. The organizers did not take this route. Their experience showed that if a neighborhood were given benefits aside from any efforts of their own, they had no sense of ownership or empowerment. The people would continue to feel disenfranchised and victimized.

Instead, the Piedmont leadership arranged for discussion groups among people not normally in relationship with one another. In fact, the organization was so successful in empowering blacks and whites together that they came under attack from the Klan for taking away so many potential converts from the white supremacy movement.

The organization held classes ranging from literacy to local government and registered people to vote. The community-building process was time-consuming and labor intensive, but it was lasting. Not only was the campaign to obtain the dumpster a success, but when the citizens finally got their dumpster, rather than signaling the end of a campaign, it signaled the beginning of many more community efforts. When the people involved trusted themselves, believed in themselves, and were in turn entrusted and believed in, a sense of community arose, an empowered community. *Empowerment* is an emergent quality that is quite a blow to a mindset that values hierarchy. On the one hand, hierarchy depends on the understanding of the one for the many: Only the one is empowered, and that power is externally bestowed, such as in the case of a king. On the other hand, emergence depends on the understanding of "the many" to form "the one"—community. In this case, the many are empowered from within. Paradoxically, then, empowerment is a humbling experience. According to contemporary theologian Carter Heyward, humility is "a sign of our common humanity. . . . To be humble means to know ourselves as no more or less valuable than anyone else in the world."[22] In fact, *humility seems to be a prerequisite to emergence.*

Another distinguishing factor is that *emergence is not a matter of smooth progression.* On an evolutionary scale, there may be movement in one direction and then a stopping or a dying out. There may be long periods of equilibrium. There may be small changes and drastic leaps.

But once the leap is taken, the more complex form provides the "purpose" for the simpler forms, while the simpler forms provide the "mechanisms."[23] For instance, in the human body, the complex circulatory system provides the purpose for the heart, and the "simple" heart provides the mechanism for the circulatory system.

Furthermore, the more complex cannot be reduced to the simpler forms without destroying the emergent qualities.[24] To put it another way, we cannot reduce water to hydrogen and oxygen without losing the quality of a liquid.[25] This is one of the characteristics of emergence: *We cannot reduce the whole to its parts without losing the emergent qualities of the whole.*

The question arises as to whether the emergent qualities are a matter of "adaptation" or a matter of "attraction." Does a community of organisms "adapt" to its environment in a way that by chance results in greater complexity? Or is the community of organisms "attracted" to a pattern of a more complex life form, which allows it to emerge in order to sustain itself?

Scientists from within the Newtonian worldview tend to see the unfolding of community "as a result of individuals within the community myopically optimizing their own ends and not as collective agreement toward a common goal."[26] In short, they believe that emergence happens as a result of adapting to circumstances that come by chance. They see the successful adaptation of an organism as the chance result of random and mindless trial-and-error efforts. A need arises, but any cooperation toward meeting that need is only accidental.

The element of chance in such a mindset seems to me to be a rather extreme position.

> The probability that human intelligence developed all the way from the chemical ooze of the primeval ocean solely through sequences of random mechanical processes has been recently aptly compared to the probability of a tornado blowing through a gigantic junkyard and assembling by accident a 747 jumbo jet.[27]

Controversial physicist Brian Swimme disagrees with the "chance" theory and believes there is an organizing principle at work that he calls "allurement."

You do not know what you can do, or who you are in your fullest significance, or what powers are hiding within you. All exists in the emptiness of your potentiality, a realm that cannot be seen or tasted or touched. How will you bring these powers forth? How will you awaken your creativity? By responding to the allurements that beckon to you, by following your passions and interests. Alluring activity draws you into being, just as it drew the star into being. Our life and powers come forth through our response to allurement.[28]

For Swimme, allurement is not simply a force external to ourselves, but a pattern enfolded within us that resonates with a greater pattern beyond us. Perhaps allurement is a sense of coming home, honing in on a familiar pattern that is "within," resonating with that which encompasses us. Perhaps we are involved in a relationship with a larger Pattern, or Image, that is not a matter of something confined within us, nor reducible to one individual corporate being. It seems quite possible that all of creation is indeed in a relationship that *resonates* with a greater "Pattern" or "Image" or "Force" that is reflected within itself, just as the fractals in the Mandelbrot set reflect patterns within patterns.

This Pattern calls forth all of our infinite possibilities in ways that resonate in relationship with that Pattern or Image. I agree with Brian Swimme's assertion that the key to this resonance is through our exuberance, our greatest joy, that which compels our hearts. Imagine the possibilities of emergence if the motivation were to resonate in a Relationship that was each person's greatest joy or deepest longing!

Even the earth's atmosphere struggles ceaselessly to maintain a balance that sustains life. Brian Swimme provides another vivid example:

If the concentration of oxygen were increased by only several percentage points, the conditions would become such that a single lightning strike could turn an entire forest, an entire continent, into flames.[29]

By the same token, if there were just a little bit less oxygen, we would not have the support necessary for the more complex life forms. This is only one example of how the simplest parts of the globe affect the more complex, how simpler parts seem enfolded into the larger pattern of being. According to Swimme,

> This is astonishing, truly; but we need in particular to think of those little microorganisms that produced the oxygen. How did they know to stop? They knew nothing of the macrostructure of the biosphere. They knew only their own allurements in the midst of their own unseen shaping powers. The whole Earth system was present in the microorganism.[30]

Regardless of whether we look at emergence as the result of following a pattern by chance or by allurement, what the new sciences are saying is that reducing the universe into its component parts cannot explain emergence. Emergent qualities are the result of organisms and their environment entering into complex interrelationships, or mutual relationships,[31] according to patterns of behavior. Nobel Prize laureate of physics Murray Gell-Mann concurs: "Complex adaptive systems are pattern seekers."[32]

A final characteristic of emergence is *self-organization*. Three criteria distinguish self-organizing systems: 1) availability of abundant information to all parts of the system; 2) a relationship-rich environment, that is, where relationships are primary over individual, isolated entities; and 3) self-regulation, that is, a sense of identity or consciousness or vision of some sort that regulates its behavior.[33] Like any chaotic pattern, self-organization applies not only to the physical realm, such as viewing the earth itself as an organism, but also to the social realm. As only community organizers can know, there are no shortcuts to emergence, and self-organization provides a clear example.

On the islands where I live, there was a desperate need for more affordable housing. A local group of citizens formed the Lopez Community Land Trust (CLT), rolled up their sleeves, and dared to take an initial step. They found the vision for their efforts after discovering that the CLT was a type of land reform that came out of the Civil Rights Movement. They needed the power of this vision to get through the enormous obstacles they knew lay ahead.

First, they incorporated to create the CLT. They formed a board of directors from people who had never served on a board before. They went through the laborious process of making by-laws and ground leases. They sought out experts for help, only to discover that they as citizens were treading new ground, and there was little help "out there." They trained themselves from bottom to top. The first prospective homeowners met every week for a year and a half, trained themselves in the world of finance, learned the legal lingo of their ground lease, gained skills to operate as a cooperative, and practiced communication skills, before they used the first hammer. They then mastered basic carpentry. Homeowners contributed twenty-four to thirty-plus hours a week constructing each other's homes.

The executive director of the CLT had only a high school education, and yet negotiated contracts, let bids, hired and fired staff, fund-raised over a half-million dollars, and negotiated with banks, private foundations, the federal/state/county governments, architects, lawyers, and landowners. The initial project manager, a gifted house designer with an incredibly generous spirit, seemed to keep disappearing at crucial moments, only to confess later that he was dying of AIDS. The first boards of directors continued to have a large turnover, only to emerge into one of the hardest working and committed boards that experts in other traditional forms of affordable housing had ever seen.

Vacationers would drive by the home-building project, become intrigued, and finish their vacation working on the project. Students in architecture interned with the project. The elderly offered help in everything from serving lunch to wiring the homes for electricity. There was a long line of volunteers and a short line of paid staff.

In the end, the effort was a premier project on the West coast in the area of affordable housing and was featured in *The New York Times*. Today, the new homeowners not only have their own homes, they are more deeply incorporated into the community: They vote, serve on county-wide committees, sustain better jobs, volunteer to help their neighbors, plant beautiful vegetable and flower gardens, and engage with people in ways they never dreamed possible.

Abundant information was made available to all concerned. There was an immense emphasis on relationships, with homeowners, architects, bankers, board members, and the total community. Resonance with a greater vision, whether by the homeowners, the CLT, or the many volunteers, sustained this enormous effort. Members of this community viewed this emergence of community as nothing short of a miracle. This group had learned the Cloudhand.

In summary, emergence is the unfolding of the simple to the complex in response to an existing need for further function. Emergence seems to happen "in the dark," unobserved, until, resonating with a pattern or quality of relationship, the quantum leap occurs. There is no going back, as we would lose what we gained. Nor can we logically look back upon the process of emerging properties and articulate exactly what was the cause or how it happened. Nor can we look forward to predict what is yet to emerge.

The only thing we can predict is that there will continue to be times when individual, generally indistinguishable, characteristics will bond together in certain communal relationships that, unseen and without warning, will leap or emerge into a new, more complex form of being. And we do know that there will be recognizable patterns to this unfolding.

Emergence is not easy and not to be experienced without effort. The effort comes not in force, not in working harder, but in working differently. It is not an easy task to face our fears, to recognize our limitations, and to trust each other's unique chaotic paths. It is not easy to remember to communicate information, to value relationships over control, and to keep the vision.

Much of this effort is accomplished on faith, in the obscurity of the moment, in response to a need, in a way that resonates somehow deep in our beings. This process involves the recognition of greater needs, greater dimensions, greater complexity. Not until we truly see our limitations, and acknowledge our needs, can we open the way to solving our dilemmas. In the very act of recognizing our limitations, a new truth emerges. The problem is that it is almost impossible to acknowledge our shortcomings when we have no hope, no faith. Courage, or faith, or imagination—the daring to dream, in the full awareness of our shortcomings—is crucial to the emergence of community.

THE

CRISIS

OF

CHRISTIANITY

As the Vietnamese Buddhist monk Thich Nhat Hanh so aptly stated in a lecture I attended years ago in Seattle, "When we look at our hands, we cannot help but see our mother and father in them. We cannot deny that legacy. What we must do is foster the best of that legacy and heal the rest."

Nhat Hanh went on to say that Americans who desire to be Buddhist can never be anything but American Buddhists. Like it or not, we cannot deny our Jewish/Christian cultural heritage. Whether we are atheist, New Age, Christian, Buddhist, American Indian, or Muslim, if we have been raised within Western civilization, we have been influenced by the Jewish/Christian cultural heritage that has dominated Western world belief systems since the time of the Roman emperor Constantine. Just as Carl Jung said he had never met a North American that did not have an Indian in his psyche, those of us raised in the Western world cannot deny the Christianity lurking in our psyches. We need to look at this influence in a conscious way in order to bring forward the best and heal the rest.

The Western world is in crisis, in need, and struggles between paradigms. Crucial to this struggle is a crisis of belief, a crisis of faith in the face of the unknown unfolding. People who dare to explore the new paradigm find prevalent understandings of Christianity to be vastly inadequate, even obsolete. Rather than becoming atheists, however, people tend to be more interested in a spiritual journey that may not necessarily be religious. They are attracted to Buddhist, American Indian, Celtic, African, and other forms of indigenous spirituality. Each of these spiritual forms, however, has roots in the cultures of their own origin. We cannot pull out these spiritualities by the roots to transplant them for our own needs without tearing out a piece of the ground from which they sprang. I have studied Zen and other forms of Buddhism, along with several forms of indigenous spirituality from America, Africa, and Australia, only to find that they clarify, inform, and transform my Christian understanding (in fact, they have changed my life in the most profound of ways), but they have not made me a Buddhist or Indian or Aborigine.

Other people respond to this crisis of belief by clinging ever more rigidly, fundamentally, and some even violently, to their old hierarchical understandings. The Christian Church has quite a legacy of exterminating those with different worldviews, whether through the Inquisition, the Crusades, colonialization, or witch hunts. The same is true of other religions that thrive in the Newtonian mindset. Fundamentalist Muslims, Jews, and Buddhists have also become very rigid and often violent, with terrorism and martyrdom being acceptable fare for daily life.

The attempt to hold on to the familiar at all costs rather than embark upon the unknown, into untraveled territory, is understandable but detrimental. Like the state of "normal science," the state of "normal religion" is dependent on its doctrine and dogma, on the logical constructs developed from early experiences within a former worldview. Normal religion is a re-presentation of a former time or event, which if believed without being experienced with a similar "Aha!" in our own context, may become idolatry. If, however, a new dimension of understanding that goes beyond current definitions of religion is experienced as a knowledge-event, as an "Aha!," then we have reached a paradigm shift.

Paradigm shifting demands a great deal of courage, or faith. It is not necessary to discard the former normal religion, but it is important to see its limitations. A paradigm shift does not necessarily mean a rejection of what has gone before, but it does involve a new dimension of understanding. This new dimension focuses not on the content of religion, but on the patterns of *relating* to this new understanding, this new way of being in the world. Just as "pattern ethics" shifts our focus from set rules to patterns of relationships, perhaps religion is also maturing from a state of "normal religion," with its rules and doctrine, to a paradigm-breaking spiritual experience according to discernible patterns. *What if Christianity were intended to have been a call to a pattern of living, a pattern of relating, rather than to a content of behavior, to particulars, to specifics?*

Paradoxes, the precursors of paradigm-breaking spiritual experience, predominate within traditional Christianity. Some are very painful paradoxes. For instance, in a global community growing smaller by the minute, able to communicate by phone, e-mail, and image instantaneously, regularly, and relatively cheaply anywhere in the world, Christians are confronted with the futility of taking denominational and faith barriers very seriously, especially in areas of great human need and conflict. Denominationalism and faith restrictions begin to look more and more petty to people who are working side by side struggling with hunger, disease, ignorance, and the consequences of war.

The Christian Church preaches that all are equal in God's eyes, and yet, paradoxically, endorses discrimination based on gender. Patriarchy, a pillar of misogynist behavior, is a driving force in the Church. The Church has made much of the fact that Jesus was a male, but has made little of the fact that he was certainly not white, not first-world educated and bred, not urban, not established, and not traditional—whether in his relationship to women or in his religious practice. Christianity continues today to extol the sacrament of marriage based upon a ceremony viewing women as property, where the woman is "given away" to a man. Sexual abuse is alarming among church members, not to mention among its clergy. Even further, discrimination along gender roles has fostered gay bashing in the shadow of the Church that preaches "love your neighbor as yourself."

Perhaps one of the greatest paradoxes is that Christian churches within the most affluent cultures suffer from ennui, a deadness of spirit, while the Christianity of struggling cultures, such as Latin America and South Africa, are thriving. Many American mainline Protestant churches are in rapid decline, while the more fringe, rigid, radical "right" churches are increasing in power.

The paradoxes abound.

Jesus himself was a paradox. We know, for instance, from cultural anthropology, that much of the content of Jesus' teachings did not originate with him. He used the folk wisdom of his time. The paradox is that from such a humble understanding came tremendous empowerment. What he brought was not so much original material as a new way of understanding, a new way of relating, a new way of being in the world. Jesus offered a very simple message in terms of content, but one that has become the basis of an infinitely complex way of unfolding in the world.

Paradox was central to Jesus' life. Jesus taught in paradox, saying that the first will be last and the last first. He sat as a king upon an ass. He used parables, which operate on the principle of paradox, to break through the "normal religion" of his time. New Testament scholar John Dominic Crossan points out that Jesus' use of the parable was not to show people how to act, nor to prescribe behavior, not even to provide examples. Rather, Jesus used the parable as a means of breaking open the worldview parameters of the hearer,[1] or what I call in popular language, as a "paradigm buster." The parable is paradox at work.

Due to the familiarity of Jesus' parables to many in the Western world today, it is easy to overlook or underestimate the impact of his use of parable for his time. For instance, in the case of the well-known parable of the Good Samaritan, it was not the example of a Samaritan doing a good deed that was significant; rather, it was the fact that a Samaritan could be good. Today a comparable example would have been for Jesus to speak of a wonderful caring parent as a gay man: "Gay man" and "good parent" is as incomprehensible a standard for some people today as "Samaritan" and "good people" was in Jesus' time. "The whole thrust of the story demands that he say what cannot be said: Good = Samaritan."[2] Crossan points out that the parable

> ... confronted the hearers with the necessity of saying the impossible and having their world turned upside down and radically questioned in its presuppositions. . . . *Just so* does the kingdom of God break abruptly into a person's consciousness and demand the overturn of prior values, closed options, set judgements, and established conclusions.[3]

Most of Jesus' parables concerned this concept of the "Kingdom of God." According to the renowned scholar Norman Perrin in the text *The New Testament: An Introduction*, "there is no doubt that the proclamation of the Kingdom of God is the central aspect of the message of Jesus."[4] Actually, the term "Kingdom of God" in common usage among traditional Christians is an inadequate translation of a much more radical concept. Jesus meant the term "Kingdom of God" to convey a way of life where God's will predominates.[5] For Jesus, the coming of the Kingdom of God was in essence a paradigm shift to a new dimension that we can perhaps grasp more fully in the words of Martin Luther King, Jr.: the coming of the "Beloved Community."[6]

Jesus struggled to enable people to see with new eyes. He was offering a message that was all but incomprehensible to the prevailing mindset. The coming of the Beloved Community meant turning the prevailing worldview upside-down, jolting the people into radical questioning.

New Testament scholar Norman Perrin speaks to this paradigm-breaking quality of Jesus' teaching method:

> As the message of Jesus these [teachings] are not radical demands but part of the proclamation of the Kingdom of God. They challenge the hearer, *not to radical obedience, but to radical questioning.* They jolt him . . . [7]

Jesus knew that a change of worldview was rarely the result of logical, analytical thought. His teachings were not dependent on logical constructs because such constructs cannot communicate the as-yet-unknown. Our fears of the unknown are what trigger denial, deep feelings, and rationalizations. These prevent us from experiencing another dimension of seeing. In order to bring something radically new, Jesus needed to help his people see with another dimension. His parables called those who would listen, not to prescribed behavior, but to a new way of relating in the world. He offered not so much directions by which to map out our lives—with isolatable, chunks of information—but rather a call to the movement and direction of our lives, to relationship, to a dance of paradox, to the unfolding of each of our Belovedness.

> What happens when one is confronted by the demand to conceive the inconceivable, to say what cannot be said? Either the demand is rejected, or the person concerned begins to question all that he has taken for granted up to that moment. He is confronted by the necessity suddenly to reexamine the very grounds of his being, by a challenge that is effective at the deepest level of existential reality.[8]

The point of Jesus' message was to free people to live the unfolding of their own lives in their infinite complexity in the face of overwhelming poverty, oppression, and violence. He did not provide people with dogma or specific footsteps to follow, but revealed to us what had never been dreamed possible: a way of being in loving relationship, a way of being empowered in the unfolding of our uniqueness.

Jesus never intended for people to copy him or mimic his behavior, or to model themselves on him. This would be merely another form of idolatry, a re-presentation of someone else's experience. His goal was much more radical. He wanted people to experience the Sacred themselves—with the same fear of death and ridicule that he faced—not as something sanctioned by external authorities but as an experience that would have its own authority. The authority of Jesus was based on a very direct, intense, personal experience of being in relationship, a relationship equally available to any other human being.

Jim Douglass in his book *The Nonviolent Coming of God*

argues convincingly that the phrase "Son of Man" better translates as "human being" or child of humanity.[9] Douglass believes that Jesus saw himself as one child of humanity among many others. This is a much more humble understanding of Jesus than what we have traditionally been taught. Douglass asserts that Jesus' entire existence provided a living example of humility, where no one was valued more or less than another. Jesus' message impacted the illiterate, peasant culture of his time not so much by what he said as by what he did with his life. He lived out his belief that humility is a hallmark of the Beloved Community, and by so doing, led ordinary people on their own spiritual journey, into their own apprehension of the Sacred.

Jesus dealt on the most practical level, not with an esoteric idea in the sky. He was responding to the very real crisis in his community. There was an urgency to his "paradigm busting." He foresaw the crushing of the Hebrew people, his people, in armed revolt against the overpowering Roman empire if the tide of events were not turned. If the people continued to look to "power-over," or to any concept of hierarchy to save them or rescue them,[10] they would be destroyed. Jesus had come to show them a way that took each person seriously, that respected everyone's role. He was confident that if each person took his or her unfolding seriously, and valued each each other's unique path no more nor less than another's, the Beloved Community would emerge in their very midst.

For Jesus, the Beloved Community was not a matter of an "other-worldly" existence. Nor was the Beloved Community a matter of something within, a psychological event. Jesus went further, saying that the Beloved Community is a tangible day-by-day event that is *within our power*.[11] Jesus offered his people a way out of the impending destruction, through the power of Beloved Community. He called for a radical emergence of community in the midst of great need. He risked his life on it. Contemporary New Testament scholar Richard Horsley states that

> Jesus' healing and exorcisms were not signs that the Kingdom of God was soon to come, but indications that the Kingdom was already present.[12]

> The old order was in fact being replaced by a new social-political order, that is, the "Kingdom of God," which Jesus was inviting the people to "enter."[13]

Even the apocalyptic forecast of destruction was grounded in day-to-day experience. Apocalypticism did not refer to the end of time; it was not a "once and for all" event. Apocalypticism meant merely the coming of the Beloved Community "at last."[14]

Some people think the tragedy of Jesus resides in his death. We cannot even begin to fathom today the impact of such a degrading and humiliating death as the Roman crucifixion.[15] The death of Jesus, however, was not as tragic a loss as the near extinction of his life's work and message precipitated by the destruction of Jerusalem forty years later.

In 70 C.E., the very consequence that Jesus' message of the Beloved Community had been meant to avoid came about: The world of the Hebrew people came literally crashing down with the destruction of the walls of Jerusalem. The destruction of the Temple meant the destruction of the Hebrew worldview, forever changing Judaism—and thus, Christianity.

As the Hebrew leadership scurried to hold on tightly to the last remnants of Judaism, they tightened the standard for what they considered acceptable belief. The more orthodox Jewish brothers and sisters ostracized the Christian Jews, whom they perceived as not quite Jewish enough in content. As a result, Jesus' following became almost exclusively that of the urban Gentile or Gentile-acculturated Jew, a culture far different from that of Jesus' rural Galilee or other parts of rural Israel.

The impact of this time must not be underestimated. Under the leadership of Paul, among others, Jesus' parables began to be translated for the urban Gentile culture as analogies, which weakened their power immensely. In this more literate arena, the parables became examples subject to analysis and interpretation, a far cry from their original intention of breaking worldviews.[16]

In this Gentile world, the paradoxes of Jesus were blunted. After Jesus' death, he was "re-presented" in the Gentile culture as a King, as a god/man according to a concept common to this Gentile culture.[17] This hierarchical concept meant that Jesus' real message of empowerment was obscured. His authority was actually reduced rather than enhanced. As Dorothy Day, founder of the Catholic Worker Movement in America, said about the prospect of her being made into a saint, "I don't want to be dismissed that easily." Jesus' radical demands could be dismissed if he were reduced to a class by himself. There is no doubt, regardless of the issue of Jesus' divinity, that Jesus believed each and every follower was equally capable of his pattern of being. The followers of Jesus, however, resorted to the conventional power model of a hierarchy that was common to the Roman culture of the urban coastal communities. The clenched fists won out over those daring to dance the chaos of empowerment. Jesus' real message that had taken root in a rural peasant Hebrew culture was all but destroyed.

There are currently great gaping needs within Christianity. In its traditional sense, Christianity is as inadequate for living today as the road map is for global travel. It is not, however, that Christianity needs to be abandoned or negated; the content simply needs to be put in perspective. As long as Christianity continues to focus on particulars, on specifics, it will get lost in the infinite prescription of behavior and dogma that will never cover enough territory.

As the messenger of a new worldview, Jesus recognized that following the letter of the Law was not enough. He knew that the domain of Jewish Temple Law, which by its very nature dealt with content and details, was insufficient and inadequate. He was not preoccupied with rules; he never asked people to be right. Instead, drawing on his own cultural heritage, he called people to be faithful, faithful to relationships and the Relationship.

As a Hebrew, Jesus was part of a culture that believed in the supremacy of community, not the individual, as we do in our reductionist mindset. Individual salvation was an oxymoron for Jesus' time: No Hebrew person could exist outside of their community; to be cast out of community was the ultimate punishment. God's salvation came within the context of the Beloved Community. For Jesus, relationships with one another in Beloved Community were paramount.

In a Church where hierarchy reigns, where strong ties have been made with temporal power, it has been all too easy to dismiss the real message of Jesus, a message that speaks with authority, an empowered message: Beloved Community emerges when each of us enters into significant relationships with one another. The Beloved Community acknowledges each and every unique contribution, and, equally importantly, each and every one of our limitations.

Jesus did not withhold his awareness of limitations: He forewarned the disciples prior to his death that things were going to be much worse than they already were. He told them that even his friends would turn away: Judas would betray him, Peter would deny him. And he told them that he himself was to die. The disciples, those nearest and dearest, basically denied the truth of Jesus' words. They could not bear it. They lacked the faith for such an unfolding. Even after things were every bit as bad as Jesus had said they would be, the followers could not see. Not until after Jesus' death, when the followers had gathered at the event traditionally known as Pentecost, did they realize their interconnectedness and feel a Whole emerge that was greater than the sum of their parts. Only then did they understand. Only then could they see what Jesus had been about. Only then were they empowered to move beyond themselves as a Beloved Community.

The life and parables of Jesus were a worldview-shattering event for a people in crisis. We must be careful not to over-analyze, literalize, or petrify either his words or his life. The worldview of the clenched fists are always trying to tie down what is "true" Christianity, and what is the "real" Jesus. But logic, dogma, and doctrine can never communicate a paradigm-breaking message.

In the end, I must fall back on the words of Black Elk, when he attempted to tell the story behind the White Buffalo Calf Pipe Ceremony to a group of white people whose logical mindsets were struggling with the "mythology" and history of the Indian culture. At the close of his story, Black Elk stopped and hesitated, and then concluded with the comment: "This they tell, and whether it happened so or not, I do not know; but if you think about it, you can see that it is true."[18]

A renowned Zen paradox states:

> I looked outside my door and saw that the trees are simply trees, and the mountains only mountains, the rivers just rivers.

> As I became enlightened, the trees suddenly became more than trees, the mountains more than mountains, and the rivers more than rivers.

> Later, upon even further enlightenment, I noticed that the trees are simply trees, and the mountains only mountains, and the rivers just rivers.

The paradox is that the first statement and the last statement look the same, but their *domain* is truly different. The last statement encompasses a vastly larger dimension of understanding than the first. It does not negate the original statement but embraces it in an unfolding awareness.

The original statement—that the trees are only trees and the mountains only mountains—parallels the Newtonian paradigm that the world is divisible into discernible building blocks. After all, particles are particles, and waves are waves, and atoms are the building blocks of the universe. The Newtonian mindset simply sees trees, mountains, and rivers as the sum of these individual parts.

However, in the grinding of gears between the old paradigm and the new paradigm—the situation where we find ourselves currently—we are becoming aware that the trees are *more* than trees, and the rivers are *more* than rivers. Reality is not simply a particle or wave. The whole is more than the sum of its parts. Some suggest that this "more" is magic or supernatural.

Originally, the basis of science was what we now refer to as "magic." Magic became distinguished from science only as a new scientific worldview emerged. For instance, most people today consider astrology to be magic. At one time, however, astrology was the tool of a powerful elite who carried the status of physician. Astrology was considered to be a source of great wisdom, if not healing. Perhaps the practitioners of astrology, when threatened by a scientific paradigm that dealt with specific content rather than patterns, with exactness rather than trends, became rigid, moving into exact fortune-telling to exert more control. Such a reaction could have been responsible for petrifying astrology into today's horoscope form found in local newspapers, a form it was never meant to take. In this way, astrology and other forms of "magic" could have been thwarted from maturing into the next paradigm. Fear may have resulted in clenched fists, a rigid posturing, rather than the assurance to dance the process of changing worldviews, as with the Cloudhand.

As we more fully enter the new paradigm, however, we are discovering that the "more" of the sum of the parts is far from magic. Emergent qualities such as self-organization and empowerment constitute the "more." These emergent qualities are not based on particular building blocks but on a resonance of relationship according to distinct patterns.

In the new paradigm, a tree is simply a tree not because it is made of individual solid particles—in fact, the content of the tree is ever-changing, impermanent—but because it has a pattern of organized and limited relationships of infinite possibility responding to a need. The tree has a pattern of a trunk with extending branches that stand against the sky and provide the tree with access to energy from the sun ("photovolaic"). Its roots sink into the ground where they find food and water. The tree is also enfolded in an even greater pattern of existence to which we and the tree belong. The tree's roots, along with its falling leaves or needles, enhance the soil. The tree's branches can provide us with energy to heat our homes. The tree breathes our carbon dioxide and exhales the oxygen that we need.

This, then, is the greater understanding conveyed by the Zen paradox. The third statement that the tree is simply a tree is not a return to the original statement, but more of a coming 'round again, just as in the *t'ai chi* Cloudhand movement where energy is understood never to be lost but always to constantly circle back upon itself.

Likewise, there is a coming 'round for some of the perceived "magical" approaches to life. For example, thousands of years after the development of astrology, Carl Jung developed a method of personality assessment that reveals *patterns* of behavior corresponding to the way astrology speaks of behavior patterns. Carl Jung came to his insights by studying another form of magic known as alchemy. And, in more recent times, these descriptive patterns have been further developed by two women into the Myers-Briggs test.

Some other "magical" approaches are receiving scientific attention. In the area of health and illness, for instance, herbal remedies used by medicine men, *curanderas*, and in witchcraft are being studied with renewed interest. Although concentrated pharmaceutical drugs extracted from natural herbs clearly work faster and more powerfully for specific symptoms, they also create significant other problems in the way of side effects. More and more people are turning to the herbs themselves for healing relief, acknowledging the importance of treating the entire body as a system.[1]

I am not suggesting that we go back to a time when the trees were simply trees, because there is no going back. Emergence has happened. I do not want to live without the timeliness of telephones or my computer. I do not want to depend on communication by drumming from village to village, or by Pony Express. But I do know that there is a place in the depths of my being that still responds to drum beats as surely as I do to my heartbeat. I know that I seek the ability to share thoughts as forthrightly as the seemingly telepathic Aborigines in Marlo Morgan's book *Mutant Message Down Under*.[2] The key to coming 'round is to leave room for what we do not know—which means to keep an open hand, not a clenched one. We cannot keep an open mind when we are grasping for power.

Renowned biologist and new scientist Gregory Bateson lived for years at Esalen Institute, a New Age education and retreat center, not because he believed in their work; in fact, he did not.

> The problem is not, however, entirely symmetrical. I have, after all, chosen to live at Esalen, in the midst of the counterculture, with its incantations, its astrological searching for truth, its divination by yarrow root, its herbal medicines, its diets, its yoga, and all the rest. My friends here love me and I love them, and I discover more and more that I cannot live anywhere else. I am appalled by my scientific colleagues, and while I disbelieve almost everything that is believed by the counterculture, I find it more comfortable to live with the disbelief than with the dehumanizing disgust and horror that conventional occidental themes and ways of life inspire in me.[3]

Here was a scientist daring to live the paradox, not able to let go of his own mindset lest it be seen as a regression to times of magic, and yet profoundly aware that somehow Esalen had something life-giving to offer him, which his peers, obsessed with particular facts and control, had not. Somehow his heart resonated with a deeper meaning that he was not yet able to articulate.

Bateson was in a struggle to come home to himself. Coming home to ourselves also means "coming 'round." The beauty of the new paradigm is that it is dependent upon everyone's participation. No one is to be excluded. There are no restrictions for class, gender, race. The new worldview is not dependent on "what you know" or even "who you know." It is not a matter of being right or "all together" or good. It is not a matter of having enough money or material or professional success. The emergence of the new paradigm is a matter of a gathering of individuals coming home to themselves, recognizing their limitations and needs, entering into mutually beneficial relationships, becoming empowered, and emerging into a new and more complex entity.

In such a paradigm, leaders will emerge in response to the needs, not to control but to empower. Behavior will crystallize out of an apparent vacuum into active particularities and then evaporate again. Entering the new paradigm is not a move into utopia, where we will never again make mistakes; rather, we are about to learn a way of being that will enable our survival. We do not need to know the answers ahead of time. The answers will unfold according to our needs if we dare to dream again, to let our creativity fly, to dance the unknown.

I once heard a dramatic story, told by Frei Alamiro, co-worker of Nobel Peace Prize winner Father Adolofo Perez Esquivel. Alamiro spoke of a gathering of squatters in one of the *favelas* or shanty towns outside his home city of Sao Paulo, Brazil. The local nonviolent peace and justice organization had been working with the squatters. The people of the *favela* were meeting regularly in small groups, discussing the teachings of Jesus. They were also learning to organize themselves to better their living conditions. As yet, there was no running water in their *favela*, no sewage system, nothing.

One day someone came into the *favela* and informed them of what they had overheard: In three days the military was coming to bulldoze the *favela* flat. Upon hearing this news, these poverty-stricken, and seemingly powerless, people responded. On the fateful third day, the squatters gathered, each according to their own way, on the road into the *favela*. The Jehovah Witnesses lined up with their tracts, the Mormons with their sacred book, the Roman Catholics with their saints, and the Baptists with their Bibles. They formed a human chain across the road.

The troops arrived, accompanied by dogs, ambulances, and nurses. Clearly violence was anticipated. The troops, temporarily stopped by this nonviolent human chain, camped on the *favela's* edge. Meanwhile, out of nowhere, two lawyers appeared to take the people's case to court. The lawyers needed some time.

Tension increased over the next few days. The captain of the troops grew more and more irritated. One morning he started haranguing the troops, trying to urge them to attack the *favela*. At the same time, one of the *favela* members called her young son to her. She had arranged a series of coffee cups on a tray, and she asked her son to take the Brazilian brewed coffee to all "our friends."

Just as the captain was at fever pitch exhorting his soldiers to attack, this little boy came up to him, tugged at his trousers, and said, "Mister, my mother told me to bring this coffee and share it with our friends." The captain shrugged the kid off and continued his tirade.

The little boy tugged again at the captain's pant leg, "No, sir. My mother said! She told me to bring this coffee to our friends!"

The Captain stopped his tirade, looked at the little boy, and sat down and shared coffee.

The *favela* was spared. The lawyers won the injunction.

The symbol now for nonviolence in Brazil is the coffee cup and the rifle.

The importance of this story is not that the *favela* won, though that was wonderful and needed. The importance of this story is not how to organize, though that, too, is an important lesson. The importance of this story is the radical turning 'round, the coming home of each person to play his or her part, the emergence of community within their very midst. The importance of this story lies in the direct and intimate consciousness of Beloved Community between child and soldier.

Is not emergence into community the recognition of a sense of belonging? Is not emergence the point at which this resonance is shared by each individual whereby there is mutual awareness? Is not coming home to ourselves a matter of resonating with a larger Pattern or Image or Relationship of which we are an interconnected part?

The contemporary Benedictine monk David Steindl-Rast speaks about the ultimate nature of this sense of resonance, of belonging, of "coming home":

> May I come back to the sense of belonging and of being at home? If we use the term *God* correctly—correctly meaning in the sense in which the deepest, the holiest people in all the different world traditions would use it and would agree on its

use—if you use it in that sense, we mean by God the
reference point of our belonging. The one reality to
which we ultimately belong and which therefore
most intimately belongs to us can be called God.[4]

If, as Jacques Maritain has said, "The means are . . . the end
in the process of becoming,"[5] perhaps the key to emergence is for
the means to *resonate* with the end. In other words, the means must
be consonant, or in harmony, with the ends. The means must come
'round with the ends. If our "end" is Beloved Community, then the
"means" is finding our own unique path in relationship that can
only be recognized by a sense of overwhelming resonance, of coming home. Only then will the new paradigm truly emerge among us.

During the height of the Reagan era, a group of white
women walked across this country, myself among them, along the
route of the "white train," the only train to carry nuclear weapons
in the United States. Each step was a prayer for peace on this
cross-country pilgrimage. Every twenty miles we stopped and
stayed, sharing the story of the bombing of Hiroshima and Nagasaki, as well as the story of nonviolent resistance along the route
of the "white train." Every twenty miles we met one or maybe two
people who, when warned that the nuclear train was about to move
through their towns, went out and met the train, witnessing with
signs, candles, and prayer. Each of these local citizens shared with
us that they felt silly and alone. They saw themselves only as isolated
individuals. Over time, we began to meet some of the train engineers, and the engineers spoke of seeing *every* twenty miles people
watching their train, with candles, and songs, and even kneeling in
prayer! These engineers said that this witness struck them to the
very core of their being. We shared the stories of these lonely vigilers
and the impact of their witness on the train crews with more and
more people whom we met along the tracks.

In the deep South as we continued walking, we became
discouraged. Word of the "white train" had not gotten out in this
isolated, poverty-stricken, rural area. We met intense hostility from
the white Christian community. Over and over again, the black
churches opened up their doors to us white women walkers.

One local woman, a retired domestic and the only black

member of a little southern Catholic church, took us walkers aside and said, "Don't listen to them folks. They tell you what you are doin' is silly—that it don't do no good. Well, let me tell you—that is what they told me when we was sittin' in at the 'whites only' lunch counters. And today, I can stay in a motel if I need to, and I can eat at any restaurant while I'm on the road if I need to. I don't have to sleep cold and hungry in my car."

The next day as we were walking, she pulled up beside us on the road with another of her unique gifts, the biggest four-layer chocolate cake we had ever seen.

Two days later another black woman took us young white women walkers aside and said, "You white people are funny. If you go up to the door and knock, and no one opens the door, you get discouraged, or angry. You start to pound on that door until your knuckles are bloody. Sometimes you just go ahead and blow up that door. Now me, if I can't get anyone to open that door for me, I step back and I look around. I climb a tree, climb over a wall, wade a stream, weave a web, and sooner or later I'm on the other side of that door." And she was.

Through the work of the train vigilers, the nuclear train eventually stopped running westward. The emerging resistance to the "white train" resonated to such an extent with people all across the country that the government secretly started transporting the nuclear weapons by truck. The once "white train" stopped running altogether in the U.S., and finally was scheduled to go to the former Soviet Union to carry their nuclear weapons to disassembly sites.[6]

The point of these stories is not that the "white train" was stopped, however, or that the transport of nuclear bombs was not stopped. The point is that some very independent, imperfect, and widely divergent people recognized their limitations and entered into relationship, and empowered community emerged. Such community was and is terrifying to those who are in control. Do not ever doubt that the emerging of community or a new paradigm will meet resistance, even violent resistance, as we have seen so poignantly in the civil rights struggles in the United States.

Ernesto Cardenal, priest and enabler of a revolution in Nicaragua, has been very involved in the *comunidades de bases* movement in his country. These Christian communities are an amazing example of grass-roots empowerment. He published a book in the form of a long poem, a beautiful mystical expression called the *Cántico Cósmico* ("Cosmic Canticle") that was inspired by the poetry of the lives of those with whom he has been enmeshed. The poem contains a tremendous outpouring of the Spirit.[7] I was reminded that this great poem of praise was written by a person who had been part of a revolution that had just met a stunning defeat at the hands of a political party put in power by the United States.

When Cardenal was asked how he and his cohorts were dealing with the defeat of their political party, he responded that they had wept, but that they knew deep in their hearts their loss verified that a true democratic revolution had taken place. Cardenal pointed out the paradox that only a truly democratic revolution would have allowed the possibility for winners and losers, since only a dictatorship can guarantee itself a win. They had allowed the space for such a loss. The spirit of the revolution had been allowed to ring true, and they would continue to hold out the hope that democracy would prevail.

The spirit behind the *Cántico Cósmico* is not the spirit of winning, but the spirit of "the means are the end in the process of becoming," or as in the Spanish rendition, "we make the road by walking it." This is an entirely new mindset, another way of being, another way of seeing, and it empowers in the oddest places. Winning is not the focus; control is not the point. The point is each of us being able to come home to ourselves in a way that resonates with a greater Pattern that draws us into further states of emergence. The new paradigm offers the hope, the faith, that in the face of the very worst, something creative will emerge to overcome it.

At one time, I lived at a Catholic Worker House of Hospitality for homeless women and children that I had co-founded. Several of the staff of the Catholic Worker House were recruited as peacekeepers for a rally protesting the Trident submarine stationed in the area, a submarine capable of destroying 408 cities, or dropping the equivalency of 2040 Hiroshima bombs.

At the same time, I had a part-time job as a cook at a nearby convent. One day I casually mentioned to one of the nuns who had befriended me at the convent that I had discovered our phone at the Catholic Worker House was tapped. When I said that I presumed it was the result of our work in opposition to the Trident submarine, I saw her face shatter like a mirror. The struggle was obvious. I had shattered her worldview. If she were to believe me, either her country was not what she had thought, or I was not the person that she had thought, that is, a "good" person. She decided to recover the pieces of her more familiar worldview and never spoke to me again.

When we receive information that shatters our worldview, rather than dare to find the new, we often flee into denial, or minimalization. It takes a tremendous act of courage to dance the unknown.

Brian Willson demonstrated this courage when he sat in front of a train headed to deliver weapons to Central America to kill innocent men, women, and children, and a few revolutionaries (guerrillas, they were called). The train that Brian was facing increased speed, rolled on, refusing to stop. It severed one of Brian's legs and so badly mauled the other that it, too, had to be amputated.

Brian was a Vietnam War vet. He had seen first-hand the horror our government was capable of inflicting. He had also visited Nicaragua where he had seen women and children with limbs amputated by weapons supplied to a para-military group by the U.S. government. His heart had been wrenched. He had walked to accompany these peasants on their turf, on their land, risking stepping on land mines himself, to protect and protest the damage done to these people he loved.

When Brian returned to this country, his home, he found he could not sit idly by and watch those trains with weapons headed to kill the people he loved. He could not remain silent. He knew many of the American people knew the truth, but the silence was deafening. By daring to sit in front of the train carrying those weapons, Brian refused to let us ignore what we were doing. He made visible what we dared not think. He exposed our denial for the sake of his Beloved Community.

Brian did not have a death wish; he did not want to lose his legs. But Brian could not live with the complicity. He brought reality to our breakfast table. He stood in solidarity with a new way of seeing, a new way of being, a radical shift of values.

Brian's act was not a rational act, but it was an act of the heart. It was not an act for us to mimic or copy. It was an act of sheer poetry, as paradigm-busting as any parable. It was an act that shatters our worldview, whether we dare to acknowledge that fact or not. It was an act that crystallized out of nowhere and evaporated again, but the reverberations are still being felt. Though it was most definitely Brain's act, it was an act that is now a part of each of our lives. It was the act of someone committed to a greater resonance, a greater sense of interconnectedness, of hope, of belonging.

People like Brian who live their faith out of a direct, intimate consciousness of belonging, of being beloved, of seeing the world in an entirely different dimension, of resonating within an Ultimate Relationship, provide the witness of community emerging in our midst. These people provide the awareness that losing and death do not have the final say. As one of my mentors, a clown named Ken Feit, once said, "It is not death we must fear, but deadness."

This is not to say that people who dare to enter the new paradigm will be tested by death. In reality, most of us will only be tested by our *fear* of death, whether physically, professionally, or materially. More pertinent, these examples show us that even the worst—death—need not be feared. The witness of thousands of people sentenced to death by AIDS reveals that even when a future of certain death is known, we can still dare to live. However, as one of my priest friends has poignantly observed, most of us "make a dying" rather than "make a living."

One person who chose to "make a living" comes vividly to mind. I was privileged to interview a professor at the Harvard Divinity School during my return to academia in Cambridge. He was a man who combined a Ralph-Nadar-understanding of the world with faith development. He organized a conference on theology and the environment with Al Gore as keynote speaker. He was married with three children. He was also an active Episcopal priest. I had great admiration for this professor/priest. Recently I discovered in a newspaper article that he had decided to run for political office, that is, for lieutenant governor of the state of Massachusetts. I also learned he was a hemophiliac and HIV-positive. I both wept at the tragedy and rejoiced that a person sentenced to early death dares to live his heart's unfolding.

We do not need to know the answers, know the future, or control the path in order to live. Religion or spirituality or faith is not a matter of such things. However, faith, of whatever particular manifestation, does supply the courage necessary to enter a new paradigm. Surviving the crisis of our times is not a light challenge, nor an easy one. And yet the answer is as simple as coming home to ourselves, resonating with that greater whole of which we are but an interconnected part, and at some unknown instant, emerging into a new way of being with one another.

If we are true to our personal, unique unfolding, coming home to ourselves in as concrete down-to-earth manner as we are capable, we can discover great joy in living. The paradox of the new paradigm lies in the fact that at the moment we find our deep fulfillment, our well of vitality, even our joy, we also find the means to serve, to offer our unique gift to the rest of our community. Perhaps Frederick Buechner says it best: "The place God calls you to is the place where your deep gladness and the world's deep hunger meet."[8]

The world is alive with people living their unfolding, most of whom will never be noticed by any historian, newspaper, or institution. These people resonate with a calling forth beyond themselves in response to a need that they dare to acknowledge. They are the future, practicing the Cloudhand dance. May each of us be equally as bold.

*S*he came from another land—Greenham Common was its name. She was a housewife, and she looked like one. She began by chaining herself to the statue in the middle of the square in her little town in England near Greenham Common. Then, she took her child's carriage and marched to the American cruise missile base with other mothers. Finally, she joined other women and formed a peace camp—the first one. She came to tell her story to others, to us in the desert, and we listened, and were infected by her testimony.

Some of us turned to one another and said, "Ah yes, let us do the same . . . "

"No," said other members of the group, "you'll ruin the peace movement here. You'll ruin our credibility!"

So, we waited. Two more weeks.

"No, you'll ruin the peace movement here," they said again.

And two of us, a man and a woman, looked at each other and said, "We've heard this before," and set the date for the founding of our own peace camp.

On a summer morning at 5:30

a.m., before the heat had begun to rise on the desert sands, but only by minutes, six of us gathered with our signs, primitive at best—"Yes to Life, No to Cruise"—just outside the only military base in the world where people were trained to use the ground-launched cruise missile. We had a plastic tarp rigged against the omnipresent sun, one little tent, four or five sleeping bags, and hearts full of vision of another way.

The winds came up. Four times our little shelter bit the dust that first day. Our leaflets had to be weighted down with piles of rocks. The workers at the cruise missile training base came and went. Someone brought us supper. At the end of the day, when it was time for bed, we dared to believe that we were not going to be arrested. We had not been arrested! My god, order a "Port-o'-Potty"! The camp had begun.

Week one. Word drifted in to us that the base security, as well as locals, figured we would die in the summer sun, so why bother with removing this batch of riff-raff: a hippy, an ex-nun, a lesbian, a welfare mom considered crazy, a housewife, and the son of a Marine colonel. Meanwhile, there were some ominous gatherings at the "Road-to-Ruin Bar" across the street that kept supplying the nerve "on tap" to soldiers of the base. Yet a few of the soldiers would drop by when the bar closed at midnight to tell us what it was like to sit in Titan missile silos.

One night we awoke to a stockinged figure in black, whose knife had just slit open each of our tents, and in whose hand was . . . oh, good, a water balloon, not so dangerous a weapon. Time to set a "watch." Two old "commies," refugees from the McCarthy era, one blind but with excellent ears and the other with excellent eyes, volunteered to take watch one night a week. A retired copper miner came another night. A farm labor organizer for Chavez took another night's watch.

The daylight crowd of protesters joining the campers began to grow, and included children, even children who wrote poetry. Supper kept coming, day by day. Oh, and word came sifting in with the dust that the military was having second thoughts about our being there.

The base offered us a deal. If we would move five hundred feet closer to the base, they wouldn't bother us. What? Closer???

(Of course we knew that bulldozers would be tearing up that area for a road—we had done our homework—but we also knew that the move would give us one more month of existence.) We jumped at it.

Then we began the first demonstrations. Six women volunteered to walk onto the base with roses and children's toys. Henrietta Thoreau, a sixty-year-old organizer from the League of Women Voters, was the first woman arrested. She nearly fainted from fear, but she left the base beaming.

We established "Blunder in for Facts" (BIFF—not FBI) as our central intelligence agency. When our "hippy" wandered around the camp and found a photograph blowing in the sand, he picked it up. It was a security photo that had been passed out to alert the guards as to who one of the the prime trouble-makers was. This trouble-maker was one of those infamous women first arrested, carrying a teddy bear.

Then we planned a major civil disobedience (CD)—simple trespassing. One of the peace campers who intended to participate in the CD went to the mall with her teenage daughter. At the mall, the daughter noticed a demonstration of guard dogs from the base. When the soldier wanted the guard dogs to stop, he threw a green tennis ball and yelled, "Out!" Thus it happened that seventy civilly-disobedient citizens—patriots, we saw ourselves—carried green tennis balls when we trespassed on that base.

Six judges in that town—a town where it was legal to ride a motorcycle with a sidearm on your hip—said to the trespassers: "I sentence you to a Merry Christmas;" "community service;" "community service wherever you want, even your anti-nuclear group;" "case dismissed;" and "did you know that some of the greatest steps in civil rights have come as the result of civil disobedience? No one in my court will go to jail for trespassing, but you must do community service."

The ranks were growing. The newspaper carried stories regularly. We noticed that one of the faithful reporters left the local paper to become a writer for *Sojourners*, a national progressive Christian periodical of conscience.

One night the "watch" discovered two men, formerly seen at the "Road-to-Ruin Bar" and overheard talking about the Vietnam

War, crawling on their bellies across the desert toward us. We were all alerted, and with our best nonviolent voices, we called out, "Can we help you???????"

The road was coming. Once again the peace camp was moved. A narrow strip of ground between a drainage ditch and the speedway was found across the way.

The demonstrations continued. Consensus within the peace movement was tried, and tried. The "commies" didn't want the lesbians clowning in the parade. The Christians didn't want the lesbians doing anything in the parade. The women's groups didn't want the men in their parade. The New Age group wanted everybody trained just so.

Warm, dead bleeding rabbits were thrown into the camp at us. Beer bottles were thrown from the road. A pickup careened through the middle of the camp on two wheels, missing one camper literally by six inches. During the prime daylight hours, we followed the shade and vegetated while the heat crackled. We spoke nothing. No one came by. We tuned down our bodies and awarenesses to a crawl. The ground was so hot that the ensolite pads we used acted as "pot holders" to protect us from the heat. The winds continued to whip—one dust devil after another. Finally, the rains came, and then the flash floods. Add to the recipe for poor health the car exhaust. . . . Ah, but meals continued to arrive. A taxi driver even stopped at three in the morning once a week to deliver donuts and coffee to the "watch."

One morning, the city manager and two bodyguards walked up to our dusty picnic table at the encampment and asked us if we would "cut a deal." Us? For what? The base had threatened to take possession of a city road if the court did not arrest us. Therefore, the city and the peace camp jointly offered to let a local Republican county judge mediate among the peace camp, the city, and the cruise missile base. The base refused. We felt our time (and endurance) waning. A final CD was planned for the first working day of Advent.

In the wee hours of the morning, two souls, dressed in black, scared to death, climbed over the seven-foot cyclone fence topped with barbed wire. One carried a live Christmas tree, three presents, and a nativity scene. The other carried a bag of household goods: an apron, children's toys, a large ham bone, curtains, all drenched in kerosene. They also had a fire extinguisher and a large chain and padlock.

They had to traverse the length of a football field in full lighting. To run was to risk being shot. To walk was perhaps never to reach their destination. They ran, for better or for worse. When they arrived at the cruise missile building a few hundred feet from the guard house and in plain sight of the guards, they set up the tree, presents, nativity scene, along with a message to "Herod" pleading with him not to incinerate the innocents. They lit the bag of household goods in the middle of an empty concrete parking lot, leaving the fire extinguisher nearby.

Alas—and, in hindsight, thank God—they were invisible. No one saw the two shepherds of new tidings. No one saw the three-foot flames rise in the darkness. So they went and chained themselves to the cruise missile building doors, while a group gathered outside the gate singing songs into the early morning hours.

The bystanders were worried about the trespassers and suggested to the press that they call the base and find out what had happened. The base denied that anyone had trespassed, but sent security out anyway. At one point, a security guard had the trespassers full in his headlights, and they raised their hands . . . invisible . . . and he drove on. A second patrol also failed. The chained duo was finally discovered when security inside the cruise missile building tried to leave the building. The head security chief recognized their all too familiar voices. They had gotten to know one another well.

Security was in serious trouble.

The military reacted. They swept the peace camp clean, dragging campers from their last tent in the desert. No more "Port-o'-Potties." One can survive a lot of things in the desert, but not indecent exposure . . .

Once a week thereafter we kept a vigil. One cold February morning, the vigilers were sprayed with water. Yet the vigilers still came. The arrests continued. In spite of everything, El Salvadorans, Indians, lesbians, Christians with processional crosses, old communists, hippies, atheists, priests and nuns, street people, Vietnam War vets, artists, New Age folks, students—all came and found a voice in a choir that said, "Yes to Life. No to Cruise."

Federal marshals remembered us fondly. The judges talked about us. The campers never forgot the solders' stories, nor the soldiers' waves and peace signs. The military base attorney and a security sergeant struggled with their consciences over us. The county sheriffs tried to quit arresting the protesters, conveniently being on the other side of town even though they had always been forewarned.

As an aside, and only as an aside, the cruise missile dimension of the base, eight years later, closed . . .

BIBLIOGRAPHY

Alexander, Christopher. *A Timeless Way of Building*. New York: Oxford University Press, 1979.

———— and Sara Ishikawa, Murray Silverstein with Max Jacobson, Ingrid Fiksdahl-King, and Shlomo Angel. *A Pattern Language*. New York: Oxford University Press, 1977.

Anderson, Owanah. *Jamestown Commitment*. Cincinnati, OH: Forward Movement Publications, 1988.

Amrine, Frederick, Francis J. Zucker, and Harvey Wheeler, eds. *Goethe and the Sciences: A Reappraisal*. Dordrecht, Holland: D. Reidel Publishing Co., 1987.

Bateson, Gregory and Mary Catherine Bateson. *Angels Fear: Towards an Epistemology of the Sacred*. New York: Macmillan, 1979.

Bertell, Rosalie. *No Immediate Danger: Prognosis for a Radioactive Earth*. London: Women's Press, 1985.

Broad, William J. "Moving A-Arms by Rail: Can Terrorists Be Foiled?" *The New York Times* (February 18, 1992): A-8.

Buechner, Frederick. *Wishful Thinking: A Seeker's ABC*. San Francisco: HarperCollins, 1989.

Capra, Fritjof. *The Turning Point: Science, Society, and the Rising Culture*. New York: Bantam Books, 1982.

———— and David Steindl-Rast with Thomas Matus. *Belonging to the Universe*. New York: Harper and Row, 1991.

Cardinal, Ernesto. *Cántico Cósmico*. Editorial Nueva Nicaragua, 1989.

Chopra, Deepak. *Perfect Health: The Complete Mind/Body Guide*. New York: Harmony Books, 1991.

Crossan, John Dominic. "Parable and Example in the Teaching of Jesus" in *New Testament Studies*, Vol. 18, 285-307. New York: Cambridge University Press, 1972.

————. *Jesus: A Revolutionary Biography*. New York: HarperCollins, 1994.

Deloria, Vine, Jr. "If You Think About It, You Will See That It Is True." *Noetic Sciences Review*, No. 27 (Autumn 1993): 62-71.

Dillard, Annie. *Pilgrim at Tinker Creek*. New York: Bantam, 1974.

Douglass, James. *The Nonviolent Coming of God*. Maryknoll, NY: Orbis, 1991.

Eckhart, Meister. *Breakthrough: Meister Eckhart's Creation Spirituality in New Translation*. Introduction and Commentaries by Matthew Fox. New York: Doubleday and Co., Inc., 1980.

Eisler, Riane. *The Chalice and the Blade.* New York: Harper and Row, 1987.

Freedman, David H. "Concocting a Cosmic Recipe for Matter." *Science,* Vol. 254 (October 18, 1991): 383.

Fukuoka, Masanobu. *The One-Straw Revolution: An Introduction to Natural Farming.* Edited by Larry Korn. Translated by Chris Pearce, Tsune Kurosawa, and Larry Korn. Emmaus, PA: Rodale Press, 1978.

Gleick, James. *Chaos: Making a New Science.* New York: Penguin Books, 1987.

Grof, Stanislav. *Beyond the Brain: Birth, Death, and Transcendence in Psychotherapy.* Albany, NY: State University of New York Press, 1985.

Hawking, Stephen W. *A Brief History of Time.* New York: Bantam Books, 1988.

Heyward, Carter. *The Redemption of God: A Theology of Mutual Relation.* Washington, D.C.: University Press of America, Inc., 1982.

―――. *Speaking of Christ: A Lesbian Feminist Voice.* Cleveland: The Pilgrim Press, 1989.

Horsley, Richard A. *Jesus and the Spiral of Violence: Popular Jewish Resistance in Roman Palestine.* New York: Harper and Row, 1987.

Huang, Chungliang Al. *Embrace Tiger, Return to Mountain: The Essence of Tai Ji.* Berkeley, CA: Celestial Arts, 1987.

Jones, Rufus. *Studies in Mystical Religion.* New York: Macmillan, 1909.

Kauffman, Stuart. "Antichaos and Adaptation." *Scientific American* (August 1991): 79.

Keck, L. Robert. *Sacred Eyes.* Indianapolis, IN: Knowledge Systems, Inc., 1992.

L'Engle, Madeleine. *A Wind in the Door.* New York: Farrar, Straus and Giroux, 1973.

Levenson, Jon D. *Creation and the Persistence of Evil.* New York: Harper and Row, 1988.

Lewin, Roger. *Complexity: Life at the Edge of Chaos.* New York: Macmillan, 1992.

Luti, J. Mary. *Teresa of Avila's Way.* Collegeville, MN: Liturgical Press, 1991.

Margulis, Lynn and Dorion Sagan. *Micro-Cosmos.* Arlington, TX: Summit, 1986.

May, Gerald. *Addiction and Grace.* New York: Harper and Row, 1988.

Morgan, Marlo. *Mutant Message Down Under.* New York: HarperCollins, 1994.

Neumann, Erich. *Depth Psychology and a New Ethic.* Translated by Eugene Rolfe. Boston: Shambhala Publications, Inc., 1990.

Nhat Hanh, Thich. *Being Peace.* Berkeley, CA: Parallax Press, 1987.

Northrop, F.S.C. *The Meeting of East and West.* New York: Macmillan, 1946, 1974.

Perrin, Norman and Dennis Duling. *The New Testament, An Introduction: Proclamation and Parenesis, Myth and History,* 2nd Ed. New York: Harcourt Brace Jovanovich, Publishers, 1982.

Quinn, Daniel. *Ishmael.* New York: Bantam/Turner Books, 1993.

Senge, Peter. *The Fifth Discipline.* New York: Doubleday, 1990.

Shilts, Randy. *And the Band Played On: Politics, People, and the Aids Epidemic.* New York: St. Martin's Press, 1987.

Sonea, Sorin and Maurice Panisset. *A New Bacteriology.* Boston: Jones and Bartlett, 1983.

Steiner, Rudolf. *The Philosophy of Freedom: The Basis for a Modern World Conception.,* 7th English ed. Translated by Michael Wilson. London: Rudolf Steiner Press, 1970.

————. *A Theory of Knowledge Implicit in Goethe's World Conception,* 3rd ed. New York: Anthroposophic Press, 1978.

Swimme, Brian. *The Universe Is a Green Dragon.* Santa Fe, NM: Bear & Co., Inc., 1984.

Thompson, William Irwin, ed. *Gaia-2: Emergence, The New Science of Becoming.* Hudson, NY: Lindisfarne Press, 1991.

Washington, James Melvin, ed. *A Testament of Hope: The Essential Writings of Martin Luther King, Jr.* New York: Harper and Row, 1986.

Welch, Sharon D. *A Feminist Ethic of Risk.* Minneapolis: Fortress Press, 1990.

Wheatley, Margaret J. *Leadership and the New Science.* San Francisco: Berrett-Koehler Publishers, Inc., 1992, 1994.

Wilczek, Frank and Betsy Devine. *Longing for the Harmonies: Themes and Variations from Modern Physics.* New York: W.W. Norton and Company, 1988.

Zajonc, Arthur. "Protestantism and Science: The Contemporary Dialogue." Unpublished manuscript, Physics Department, Amherst College (April 31, 1990).

NOTES

Prologue: An Invitation to Heart and Mind

1. Hawking, Stephen W., A *Brief History of Time* (New York: Bantam Books, 1988), 116.
2. Northrop, F. S. C., *The Meeting of East and West*. (New York: Macmillan, 1946, 1974), 21,22.
3. Freedman, David H., "Concocting a Cosmic Recipe for Matter," *Science*, vol. 254 (October 18, 1991): 383.

Chapter 1: Cloudhand, Clenched Fists, Community, and Crisis

1. Levenson, Jon D., *Creation and the Persistence of Evil* (New York: Harper and Row, 1988), xiii, 3, 12, 17, 113-14.
2. Gleick, James. *Chaos: Making a New Science*. (New York: Penguin Books, 1987), 29-30.
3. Huang, Chunliang Al. *Embrace Tiger, Return to Mountain: The Essence of Tai Ji*. (Berkeley, CA: Celestial Arts, 1987), 41-42.
4. Snow, C.P., cited in L. Robert Keck, *Sacred Eyes* (Indianapolis, IN: Knowledge Systems, Inc., 1992), 200.
5. For a good challenge and dialogue around the cultural myths of "civilizations" see Daniel Quinn's *Ishmael* (New York: Bantam/Turner Books, 1993), and Riane Eisler's *The Chalice and the Blade* (New York: Harper and Row, 1987).
6. Margulis, Lynn and Dorion Sagan, *Micro-Cosmos* (Arlington, TX: Summit Books, 1986), 15.
7. Deloria, Vine, Jr., "If You Think About It, You Will See That It Is True," *Noetic Sciences Review*, No. 27 (Autumn 1993): 66. This article was adapted from a chapter in *New Metaphysical Assumptions of Modern Science*, edited by Willis Harman and Jane Clark (Ions, 1994).
8. *Gaia-2: Emergence, The New Science of Becoming*, William Irwin Thompson, ed. (Hudson, NY: Lindisfarne Press, 1991). See the chapter "Symposium," especially pp. 239-245.
9. Planck, Max, *Scientific Autobiography*, 1968, cited in Stanislav Grof, *Beyond the Brain: Birth, Death, and Transcendence in Psychotherapy*. (Albany, NY: State University of New York Press, 1985), 13.

Chapter 2: Paradox and Paradigms

1. Thompson, Evan, "Perception and the Emergence of Color," in *Gaia-2*, 97-98.

2. Kuhn, Thomas, *The Structure of Scientific Revolution*, 1962, cited in Stanislav Grof, *Beyond the Brain: Birth, Death, and Transcendence in Psychotherapy*. (Albany, NY: State University of New York Press, 1985), 11.

3. Thompson, William Irwin, "Conclusion: Politics Becoming a Planet," in *Gaia-2*, 255-256.

4. The Berkana Institute (3857 North 300 West, Provo, Utah, 84604) was co-founded by Margaret Wheatley, author of *Leadership and the New Science* (San Francisco: Berrett-Koehler Publishers, Inc., 1992, 1994).

5. "Leadership and Self-Organizing Systems," sponsored by the Berkana Institute at Sundance, Utah (July 20-22, 1994).

6. Wilczek, Frank and Betsy Devine, *Longing for the Harmonies: Themes and Variations from Modern Physics* (New York: W.W. Norton and Company, 1988), 105.

7. Ibid., chapter 9: "Universal Chemistry (of The Battle Between Entropy and Energy)," 78-83.

8. Ibid., 275.

9. Hawking, *A Brief History of Time*, 11-12. Emphasis added.

10. Ibid., 129.

11. Bateson, Gregory and Mary Catherine Bateson, *Angels Fear: Towards an Epistemology of the Sacred* (New York: Macmillan, 1979), 14.

12. May, Gerald, *Addiction and Grace*. (New York: Harper and Row, 1988), 75.

13. Margulis, Lynn and Ricardo Guerrero, "Two Plus Three Equal One: Individuals Emerge from Bacterial Communities," in *Gaia-2*, 59. Emphasis added.

14. Swimme, Brian, *The Universe Is a Green Dragon* (Santa Fe, NM: Bear & Co., Inc., 1984), 113.

15. Gleick, *Chaos*, 38.

16. Grof, Stanislav, *Beyond the Brain: Birth, Death, and Transcendence in Psychotherapy* (Albany, NY: State University of New York Press, 1985), 13.

17. Gleick, *Chaos*, 38.

18. Grof, *Beyond the Brain*, 5.

19. See "The Two Paradigms" in *The Turning Point: Science, Society, and the Rising Culture* by Fritjof Capra (Bantam, 1982), 51-98.

20. Fukuoka, Masanobu, *The One-Straw Revolution: An Introduction to Natural Farming*, ed. Larry Korn, trans. Chris Pearce, Tsune Kurosawa, and Larry Korn (Emmaus, PA: Rodale Press, 1978).

21. Wilczek and Devine, *Longing for the Harmonies*, 137.

22. Zajonc, Arthur, "Light and Cognition," in *Gaia-2*, 126. Emphasis added.

23. Ibid., 126.

Chapter 3: On Whose Authority?

1. A biblical theme in Matthew 11:25; Mark 4:22; John 16:12-13,25; I Corinthians 13:2.

2. Grof, *Beyond the Brain*, 14.

3. "Leadership and Self-Organizing Systems," Berkana Institute. Discussion with consultant Maggie Moore.

4. Zajonc, Arthur, "Protestantism and Science: The Contemporary Dialogue" (unpublished manuscript, Physics Department, Amherst College, April 3, 1990): 27-28.

5. Ibid., 26-27.

6. Gleick, *Chaos*, 273.

7. Frank, Philipp, *Philosophy of Science*, 1974, cited in Grof, *Beyond the Brain*, 13-14.

8. Grof, *Beyond the Brain*, 13-14.

9. Kuhn, Thomas, *The Structure of Scientific Revolution*, 1962, cited in Grof, *Beyond the Brain*, 5.

10. Wilczek Devine, *Longing for the Harmonies*, 305.

11. I am indebted to Arthur Zajonc, member of the physics department of Amherst College, for his discussion of Goethe in his unpublished manuscript "Protestantism and Science: The Contemporary Dialogue," especially pp. 34-38. Another resource for information about Goethe is *Goethe and the Sciences: A Reappraisal*, ed. Frederick Amrine, Francis J. Zucker and Harvey Wheeler (Dordrecht, Holland: D. Reidel Publishing Co., 1987). I also refer you to Rudolf Steiner's *The Philosophy of Freedom: The Basis for a Modern World Conception*, trans. Michael Wilson, 7th English edition (London: Rudolf Steiner Press, 1970), and his work *A Theory of Knowledge Implicit in Goethe's World Conception*, 3rd edition (New York: Anthroposophic Press, 1978).

12. Zajonc, "Protestantism and Science," 14.

13. Ibid., 41-44.
14. Ibid., 38.
15. See Gleick, *Chaos*, 84.
16. Frank, Philipp, *Philosophy of Science*, 1974, cited in Grof, *Beyond the Brain*, 13-14.
17. Jones, Rufus, *Studies in Mystical Religion* (New York: Macmillan, 1909), xv.
18. Zajonc, "Protestantism and Science," 41-44.
19. Beede, A. McG., "Western Sioux Cosmology," unpublished paper in the North Dakota State Historical records, Bismarck, cited in Deloria, "If You Think About It, You Will See That It Is True," 63.
20. Ibid., Beede, 6-7; cited in Deloria, 63-64. Emphasis added.
21. Dillard, Annie, *Pilgrim at Tinker Creek* (New York: Bantam, 1974), 124.
22. Thompson, William Irwin, "The Imagination of a New Science and the Emergence of a Planetary Culture," in *Gaia-2*, 19-20.
23. Zajonc, "Protestantism and Science," 40.
24. Luti, J. Mary, *Teresa of Avila's Way* (Collegeville, MN: Liturgical Press, 1991).
25. Paraphrase of Genesis 37:19-20.
26. Jackson, Wes, "Hierarchical Levels, Emergent Qualities, Ecosystems, and the Ground for a New Agriculture," in *Gaia-2*, 138.
27. Bertell, Rosalie, *No Immediate Danger: Prognosis for a Radioactive Earth* (London: Women's Press, 1985).
28. Neumann, Erich, *Depth Psychology and a New Ethic*, trans. Eugene Rolfe (Boston: Shambhala Publications, Inc., 1990).
29. I am indebted to Thich Nhat Hanh in *Being Peace* (Berkeley, CA: Parallax Press, 1987), 74-79.
30. For one example see Randy Shilts' *And the Band Played On: Politics, People, and the Aids Epidemic* (New York: St. Martin's Press, 1987).
31. Planck, Max, *Scientific Autobiography*, 1968, cited in Grof, *Beyond the Brain*, 13.

Chapter 4: A Paradigm of Patterns

1. Chopra, Deepak, *Perfect Health: The Complete Mind/Body Guide* (New York: Harmony Books, 1991), 12.
2. Hawking, *A Brief History of Time*, 55.
3. Wilczek and Devine, *Longing for the Harmonies*, 131.
4. Ibid., 261.

5. Margulis and Guerrero, "Two Plus Three Equal One," in *Gaia-2*, 60-61. Emphasis added. For further information refer to the work of Sorin Sonea in Sorin Sonea and Maurice Panisset, *A New Bacteriology* (Boston: Jones and Bartlett, 1983).

6. Grof, *Beyond the Brain*, 67-68.

7. Thompson, William Irwin, "Introduction: The Imagination of a New Science and the Emergence of a Planetary Culture," in *Gaia-2*, 16.

8. Gleick, *Chaos*, 48.

9. Ibid., 94-103.

10. Illustrated in Gleick, *Chaos*, between pp. 114-115.

11. "Leadership and Self-Organization Systems," Berkana Institute. Discussion.

12. Ibid., 303-304.

13. Senge, Peter, *The Fifth Discipline* (New York: Doubleday, 1990), 94. Another exciting work linking business with the new sciences is Meg Wheatley's *Leadership and the New Science* (San Francisco: Berrett-Koehler Publishers, Inc., 1992).

14. This story of Kauffman's was told at the Berkana Institute "Leadership and Self-Organizing Systems." Further information on this work of Stuart Kauffman can be found in Roger Lewin's *Complexity: Life at the Edge of Chaos* (New York: Macmillan, 1992), pp. 23-32.

15. Alexander, Christopher, *A Timeless Way of Building* (New York: Oxford University Press, 1979), 90. For further examples of this concept, I encourage you to read Alexander's second work, a collaborative effort called *A Pattern Language* by Christopher Alexander, Sara Ishikawa, Murray Silverstein, with Max Jacobson, Ingrid Fiksdahl-King, and Shlomo Angel (New York: Oxford University Press, 1977).

16. Ibid., 67-68.

17. Deloria, "If You Think About It, You Will See That It Is True," 68-69.

18. Ibid., 63-64.

19. "Leadership and Self-Organizing Systems," Berkana Institute. Story told by Myron Kellner-Rogers.

Chapter 5: Pattern Ethics

1. Welch, Sharon D., *A Feminist Ethic of Risk* (Minneapolis: Fortress Press, 1990), 4. For further information about the concept of "universal intellect," refer to Michel Foucault, *Power/Knowledge: Selected Interviews and Other Writing 1972-77* (New York: Pantheon Books, 1980).

2. Anderson, Owanah, *Jamestown Commitment* (Cincinnati, OH: Forward Movement Publications, 1988), 19.

3. Ibid., 19-20.

4. "Leadership and Self-Organization," Berkana Institute.

5. L'Engle, Madeleine, *A Wind in the Door* (New York: Farrar, Straus & Giroux, 1973).

6. Wilczek and Devine, *Longing for the Harmonies*, 275.

7. Gleick, *Chaos*, 9-31.

8. Bohm, David, *Wholeness and the Implicate Order* (London: Routledge and Kegan Paul), cited in Fritjof Capra, *The Turning Point: Science, Society and the Rising Culture* (New York: Bantam, 1982), 95-96.

9. L'Engle, *A Wind in the Door*.

10. Douglass, James, *The Nonviolent Coming of God* (Maryknoll, NY: Orbis, 1991), 30.

11. A. J. Muste is a renowned pacifist and advocate of nonviolence.

12. Maritain, Jacques, *L'Homme et l'Etat*, cited in Douglass, *The Nonviolent Coming of God*, 154.

13. Eckhart, Meister, *Breakthrough: Meister Eckhart's Creation Spirituality in New Translation*, Introduction and Commentaries by Matthew Fox (New York: Doubleday and Co., Inc., 1980), 399.

Chapter 6: Emergence

1. Thompson, William Irwin, "Introduction: The Imagination of a New Science and the Emergence of a Planetary Culture," in *Gaia-2*, 24.

2. Margulis and Guerrero, "Two Plus Three Equal One," in *Gaia-2*, 59-60.

3. Swimme, *The Universe Is a Green Dragon*, 95.

4. Kauffman, Stuart, "Antichaos and Adaptation," *Scientific American* (August 1991): 79.

5. Gould, Jay, cited in Roger Lewin, *Complexity: Life at the Edge of Chaos* (New York: Simon & Schuster, 1992), 143.

6. Ibid., 139.

7. Ibid., 143.

8. Ibid., 141.

9. Quinn, Daniel, *Ishmael* (New York: Bantam/Turner Books, 1993), 61.

10. Lewin, Roger, *Complexity: Life at the Edge of Chaos* (New York: Simon & Schuster), 64.

11. Margulis and Guerrero, "Two Plus Three Equal One," in *Gaia-2*, 60.

12. Jackson, Wes, "Hierarchical Levels, Emergent Qualities, Eco-systems, and the Ground for a New Agriculture," in *Gaia-2*, 143. Though there is much to commend in this article, I do feel that Jackson is bound by a concept of hierarchy that is no longer useful in our understanding of nature.

13. Oyama, Susan, "Symposium," in *Gaia-2*, 240. Emphasis added.

14. Jackson, "Hierarchical Levels," in *Gaia-2*, 147.

15. Ibid., 142.

16. Swimme, *The Universe Is a Green Dragon*, 113.

17. Jackson, "Hierarchical Levels," in *Gaia-2*, 142.

18. Ibid., 143.

19. Wilczek and Devine, *Longing for the Harmonies*, 154.

20. Ibid., 154.

21. Ibid., 152.

22. Heyward, Carter, *Speaking of Christ: A Lesbian Feminist Voice* (Cleveland: The Pilgrim Press, 1989), 56-57.

23. Jackson, "Hierarchical Levels," in *Gaia-2*, 144.

24. Ibid., 146.

25. Ibid., 147.

26. Lewin, *Complexity*, 188.

27. Grof, *Beyond the Brain*, 23.

28. Swimme, *The Universe Is a Green Dragon*, 51.

29. Ibid., 137.

30. Ibid., 137.

31. For an excellent presentation of a theology of mutual relation-ship, see Carter Heyward's *The Redemption of God: A Theology of Mutual Relation* (Washington D.C.: University Press of America, Inc.), 1982.

32. Gell-Mann, Murray, personal communication.

33. I am indebted in this discussion to the work of the Berkana Institute, in particular the "Leadership and Self-Organizing Systems" dialogue.

Chapter 7: The Crisis of Christianity

1. Crossan, John Dominic, "Parable and Example in the Teaching of Jesus," *New Testament Studies*, vol. 18 (1972): 285-307, especially 304-305.

2. Ibid., 295.

3. Ibid., 295.

4. Perrin, Norman and Dennis C. Duling, *The New Testament, An Introduction: Proclamation and Parenesis, Myth and History*, 2nd Edition (New York: Harcourt Brace Jovanovich, Publishers, 1982), 413.

5. Crossan, John Dominic, *Jesus: A Revolutionary Biography* (New York: HarperCollins, 1994), 54-74. This is an excellent work for anyone interested in the socio-political ramifications of Jesus's life and times, the stories behind the stories, and the humanness of Jesus.

6. Unfortunately, the term "Kingdom of God" denotes hierarchy, not to mention geographic location. Hierarchy is simply inaccurate in describing the nature of emerging relationships, since the key concept is not hierarchy but "need." I think that the term "Kingdom of God" served its purpose at one time, but in our age "kingdom" has primarily negative associations, and if not negative, certainly other-worldly, as in the days of old with Robin Hood. We need as concrete an image for our times as "kingdom" was for the Hebrews of Scripture. Therefore, for the remainder of this work I will use Martin Luther King, Jr.'s term "Beloved Community" (*A Testament to Hope: The Essential Writings of Martin Luther King, Jr.*, ed. James Melvin Washington, New York: Harper and Row, 1986, 18) when making a parallel tie with the concept of Kingdom of God.

7. Perrin and Duling, *The New Testament*, 422. Emphasis added.

8. Ibid., 417.

9. Douglass, *The Nonviolent Coming of God*, 39-40.

10. For an excellent discussion of the intention of Jesus in speaking about the Son of Man in light of the looming destruction of Jerusalem, see Douglass' *The Nonviolent Coming of God*, chapter 5, "Jesus, Jerusalem, and the End of the World," 114-180.

11. Douglass, *The Nonviolent Coming of God*, 106.

12. Horsley, Richard A., *Jesus and the Spiral of Violence: Popular Jewish Resistance in Roman Palestine* (New York: Harper and Row, 1987), 181.

13. Ibid., 207.

14. Ibid., 168.

15. Crossan, *Jesus: A Revolutionary Biography*, pp. 123-158. This is a ruthless investigation of the art of Roman crucifixion at the time of Jesus, and not for the faint of heart.
16. Crossan, "Parable and Example in the Teaching of Jesus," 306.
17. For an excellent synopsis of this issue, consult Perrin and Duling's *The New Testament*, "Gods and Saviors," 13-15.
18. Black Elk, from John G. Neihardt, *Black Elk Speaks* (Lincoln, NB: University of Nebraska Press, 1972), 4, cited in Deloria, "If You Think About It, You Will See That It Is True," 64.

Chapter 8: Coming 'Round

1. Capra, *The Turning Point*, 348-349. I recommend this entire chapter, "Wholeness and Health."
2. Morgan, Marlo, *Mutant Message Down Under* (New York: HarperCollins, 1994).
3. G. Bateson and M.C. Bateson, *Angels Fear*, 51.
4. Capra, Fritjof and David Steindl-Rast with Thomas Matus, *Belonging to the Universe* (New York: Harper and Row, 1991), 16.
5. Maritain, *L'Homme et l'Etat*, cited in Douglass, *The Nonviolent Coming of God*, 154.
6. Broad, William J., "Moving A-Arms by Rail: Can Terrorists Be Foiled?," *The New York Times* (Feb. 18, 1992): A-8.
7. Cardinal, Ernesto, *Cántico Cósmico* (Editorial Nueva Nicaragua, 1989).
8. Buechner, Frederick, *Wishful Thinking: A Seeker's ABC* (San Francisco: HarperCollins, 1993), 119.

INDEX

ABOUT THE AUTHOR

RHEA Y. MILLER was raised in the small towns of Iowa as the daughter of a rural Methodist circuit minister. She kept moving West and now resides on an island in Rosario Strait off the coast of Washington State. Most of her background is as a social justice activist with national and international experience. She has a Masters of Divinity from the Episcopal Divinity School in Cambridge, Massachusetts. Recently, she was elected to public office to serve full-time as a county commissioner.

Photograph by John Dustrude

The Newest and Best from LuraMedia

FINDING STONE
A Quiet Parable and Soul-Work Meditation
by Christin Lore Weber

> Enter the ancient meditative practice of standing before life's mysteries. Discover healing, wisdom, power in the beauty and simplicity of this parable and reflections.

MADELEINE L'ENGLE, SUNCATCHER
Spiritual Vision of a Storyteller
by Carole F. Chase

> For all Madeleine L'Engle fans. The first-ever comprehensive study of her remarkable life, writings, philosophy, and spiritual vision.

RATTLING THOSE DRY BONES
Women Changing the Church
Edited by June Steffensen Hagen

> Renew your vision. Twenty-two women of faith boldly share their experiences, struggles, and hopes. For any woman who has ever questioned her place in the church.

SLOW MIRACLES
Urban Women Fighting for Liberation
by G. F. Thompson

> Come face-to-face with the drama. The courage. The humor. The dignity. Real stories about real women living, surviving, triumphing in America's urban core.

RAISING PEACEFUL CHILDREN IN A VIOLENT WORLD
by Nancy Lee Cecil

> Take heart and take action. An immensely practical, activity-filled, hopeful book for every parent and teacher who wants to create a safe, peaceful world for children.

WRITING AND BEING
Taking Back Our Lives Through the Power of Language
by G. Lynn Nelson

> Revive your healing, creative journey through writing. An affirming guide to soul-work through the practice of journaling. For seekers, writers, teachers, classes, and groups.

LuraMedia books are available in bookstores
or call 1-800-FOR-LURA to order.
Ask for our free catalog.